WHOSE EUROPE?

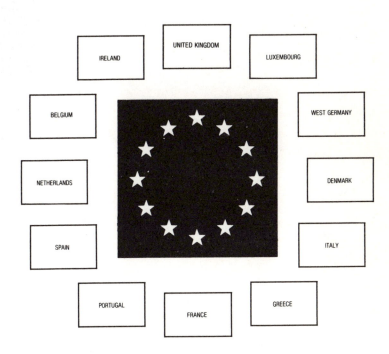

IRELAND	UNITED KINGDOM	LUXEMBOURG
BELGIUM		WEST GERMANY
NETHERLANDS		DENMARK
SPAIN		ITALY
PORTUGAL	FRANCE	GREECE

Front cover key

WHOSE EUROPE?
Competing Visions for 1992

Sir Ralf Dahrendorf · Sir John Hoskyns

Victoria Curzon Price · Ben Roberts

Geoffrey E. Wood · Evan Davis

L. S. Sealy

Foreword by
Cento Veljanovski

IEA
Institute of Economic Affairs
1989

First published in August 1989
Second Impression May 1990
by
THE INSTITUTE OF ECONOMIC AFFAIRS
2 Lord North Street, Westminster, London SW1P 3LB

© The Institute of Economic Affairs 1989

IEA Readings 29

ISSN 0305-814X
ISBN 0-255 36222-6

The Institute gratefully acknowledges financial support for its publications programme and other work from a generous benefaction by the late Alec and Beryl Warren.

Printed in Great Britain by
Goron Pro-Print Co. Ltd., Lancing, W. Sussex

Filmset in 'Berthold' Times Roman 11 on 12 point

CONTENTS

FOREWORD

Cento Veljanovski

Research & Editorial Director,
Institute of Economic Affairs

THE IEA *Readings* are designed to refine the market in economic thinking by collecting in one volume varying approaches to a theme arising from an IEA seminar or conference. *Whose Europe?* is based on papers given at the IEA conference entitled *Euro-Markets or Euro-Control*, held on 22 March 1989.

Whose Europe? continues the debate over the shape and trends in the European Community as it moves to the implementation of the Single Market in 1992.

The Treaty of Rome, which created the European Economic Community, can be seen as the 'triumph of the economics of Adam Smith'. It envisaged a free-market zone where tariff barriers and other restrictions on the free flow of goods and services, capital and peoples would be torn down.

As we approach 1992, by when the bulk of the directives constituting the Single Market programme are to have been implemented, the question is increasingly being asked: Whose Europe? The answers that have been proffered differ dramatically. There are those who believe that uniformity in institutional arrangements is required for a single market. The member-states of the Community must have the same regulations, a common currency and a European central bank, and Brussels must have the power to regulate mergers, television, financial

services and other trans-national industries and activities. This uniformity must extend beyond industrial matters to explicit regulation of
contractual relationships within and between firms. A Social Charter
has been proposed which will require, among other things, worker
representation on Company Boards and a minimum wage.

Others want to rely, in the spirit of the Treaty of Rome, on
competition and the free mobility of resources to generate increased
wealth and to create standards and regulations framed between
competitive governments offering competing jurisdictions based on the
principle of mutual recognition so elegantly dissected in Victoria
Curzon Price's Wincott Lecture published by the IEA in December
1988.[1] The harmonisation engine, according to this vision of Europe,
relies excessively on the ability of the Commission to decide for all
European nations what are the correct regulations. The European
Monetary System and a common currency would rely on the ability of
one bank to exercise monetary restraint. If there is safety in numbers, it
is surely in the regulatory field. It is only through a process of discovery
in the light of experience and against the backdrop of choice in the
ability to buy from different suppliers or locate in another country that
a regulatory framework consistent with market forces will evolve. This,
in essence, is the principle of competing jurisdictions.

The choice is, therefore, not between being European and
communautaire, or being a rampant nationalist. It is between the terms
and form that the Single Market takes and about the power and
accountability of the institutions which form the European Community, and their relationship with the rest of Europe and the world.
These tensions have always existed. In 1971 the IEA published *Rome
or Brussels ...?*[2] by Russell Lewis, who elegantly encapsulated the
competing visions of the European Community:

> 'Grossly to oversimplify, the choice for the future is between Rome and
> Brussels: between the law of a Community constitution establishing and
> reinforcing personal economic freedoms on the one hand, and a new
> European-scale version of bureaucratic, national, corporatist, over-centralist
> style government on the other.'

The IEA is an educational charity and therefore does not have a

---

[1] Victoria Curzon Price, *1992: Europe's Last Chance? From Common Market to Single
Market* (19th Wincott Memorial Lecture), IEA Occasional Paper 81, IEA, 1988.

[2] W. R. Lewis, *Rome or Brussels ...?*, Hobart Paperback No. 3, IEA, 1971, p. 5.

corporate view. The authors of the papers reproduced in this volume have all taken a critical look at recent developments in the European Community and offered their analysis of them. They present a refreshing and challenging re-evaluation of what Professor Ralph Dahrendorf calls 'the Great Debate' on the future of the European Community, a debate which will be of concern to all students, voters and Europeans.

July 1989   CENTO VELJANOVSKI

THE FUTURE OF EUROPE?

Sir Ralf Dahrendorf
Warden,
St. Antony's College, Oxford

IT IS A PLEASURE to be here under the auspices of the Institute of Economic Affairs. The 'great debate' is not yet particularly well-focussed, but it may be that a debate is beginning about the future of Europe that is more interesting and has more argument and thought behind it than has been normal. You will find in me someone who is trying to do what some might consider impossible: that is, to be a European multilateralist who believes not only that for the benefit of our economies and the lives of people in general, multilateral arrangements are ultimately preferable to regional or national ones, but also that the European Community has a role to play.

I recently reconsidered two books published in 1982 and 1988 which provide a good framework for what I shall say. The first is Mancur Olson's *Rise and Decline of Nations*, a book inspired by the 1970s in which he argues that stagflation, the bane of the 1970s, was due, in no small extent, to social rigidities which were developing almost of necessity as a result of the logic of collective action when there are long periods of stability. He was gloomy in the book, published in 1982, about the possibilities of opening up those rigidities from within. Indeed, he says—although he does not like to be reminded of it—that

'We can also appreciate Thomas Jefferson's observation that "the tree of liberty must be refreshed from time to time with the blood of patriots and tyrants".'

I am glad that Jefferson added the tyrants to the patriots and that Olson included them in his quotation. What that quotation conveys is that it is hopeless to try to open up the rigid world of, for example, the 1970s, from within. We have to await cataclysmic, catastrophic events to do that.

The Time of the Entrepreneur

From time to time Olson toys with the idea not only of revolution, which is bad enough, but of war as one of the sources of the dissolution or dissipation of the rigidities which make economic, social and political liberties so hard to defend after long periods of stability. It is a book of its time and let us remember that it was not published too soon because 1982 marked the beginning of the long boom; the beginning of a period, which is (as I put it recently, perhaps with only partial justification so far as the man is concerned) the time of Schumpeter rather than that of more administratively minded economists. By Schumpeter I mean the time of the entrepreneur rather than the manager, which had a great deal to do with the boom. While those who did not benefit as much as others during the years of the long boom have naturally complained and moaned and groaned, it is hardly the blood of patriots that has been shed in the process. It has turned out to be possible to open up a rigid stagflation and enter a period of enterprise and change.

The whole of Europe has moved out of the Euro-gloom, Euro-pessimism and Euro-sclerosis that were obvious at every conference and in every speech 10 years ago and for a few years after that.

'Signs of Competitiveness'

I turn to the second book which is Paul Kennedy's *Rise and Fall of the Great Powers*, published in 1988. It contains a strange chapter about Europe because according to his theories he should have argued that Europe can be discounted and forgotten. But he did not. In his slightly cautious way he said that there were 'many signs of competitiveness' in Europe and that Europe may go a long way. He said that there is one little problem in that there is too much diversity—everything is too dispersed. If Europeans get their act together in that respect, he says that Europe can have a considerable future.

There are six years between these two books by sensitive and important authors and that reflects in part the changing mood of the times. We should not discount the mood of the times as we talk about Europe today and 1992. We should not forget either that the mood of the times has changed quickly and it is not inconceivable that it will change again. Today there are signs in public and political debate all over Europe and beyond of a different perspective on the future than was characteristic of the past seven years. However, apart from the mood of the times, as far as the European Community is concerned this was certainly a period in which a new objective was defined effectively by the members of the European Community with the help of the Commission in Brussels and above all of its President, Jacques Delors.

It would be tempting to look in more detail at the history of the Community. I shall resist that temptation, but mention in passing that I was a Commissioner at the time when we first completed the Customs Union in the Spring of 1970. After the Hague summit in December 1969, which made a few statements that sounded rather like those made around the Single European Act, in the Spring of 1970 we solemnly declared that of the triptych that the French government had invented, *achèvement, approfondissement* and *élargissement*, the first, *achèvement*, had been attained. Now that the Customs Union was complete we could turn to other matters such as the enlargement and the *approfondissement*—the deepening of co-operation in the form of economic and monetary union.

I need not comment in retrospect either on the degree of completion of the Customs Union achieved at that time, or the fascinating debacle of economic and monetary union as planned by the European Community in 1970-71. There was a long period of relative silence from Brussels, the dreadful 1970s with all its problems, and there were times when there was no objective for the European Community. There is no more fascinating document of those times than Roy Jenkins's 1977-81 diary which shows clearly that during his entire presidency no one quite knew where the Community was or should be going. It was in the 1980s only, and even then towards the mid-1980s, that a new objective was identified. The Single Market was invented and the date 1992 was introduced into the debate. That is merely the background.

I am basically delighted about a process that is likely to lead to some extension of the famous four freedoms of the movement of people,

3

goods, services and capital or money. I hope that the process will succeed as planned.

Having said that, and to that extent set a positive tone for my following comments, there are four questions. They are sceptical and they will not be unfamiliar to you, but they need to be put time and again and to be resolved.

The Notion of the Community

The first is the obvious question of what kind of community it will be? I am sorry that the question seems to be debated, at any rate in this country, in terms of socialism or not. I do not believe that socialism is the issue anywhere in Europe—that is not what it is about. That is very much yesterday's philosophy and certainly the socialism which is attacked in public speeches is not noticeable anywhere. I do not know whether any of you have read the recent statements by the Italian communist leader, Occhetto, about the market. They are indicative of what is happening all over the world.

The character of the Community is more a question of what kind of company will dominate the process of moving towards 1992. Here I detect significant differences between some of the leading industrialists of Europe. I do not wish to produce simple classifications—it is never as simple as one makes it sound when talking about it—but there are those who have a considerable interest in public procurement and they tend to be in favour of 1992 because they hope that it will offer them further opportunities for using governments and the co-operative efforts of governments for their own benefit.

There are also those large, important companies which have managed in their own country to protect their markets to some extent and who believe that the wider European market of 1992 may enable them to use the European Community to extend that protection to a larger market. They would then simultaneously benefit from wider opportunities within the European Community and from keeping others—notably the Japanese—out. Certainly I could name several well-known European industrialists who are strong supporters of 1992 for precisely that reason and who believe that they can use the Single Market to keep others out and have their own protected playground, rather than as a stepping-stone to a wider international or multilateral arrangement that helps us return to free trade, and that might not benefit particular companies, but would ultimately benefit us all.

On the other hand, those companies that operate freely across boundaries and on a worldwide scale have many of their markets outside the Community and do not particularly care about 1992. They are not usually against 1992; they find it possible to adjust to more European co-operation just as they have found it possible to adjust to other things all over the world. They adjust their own organisation and behaviour within the markets, but they do not have a great interest in 1992. They regard it as 'one of those things'. They would not be opposed, but neither would they be strong supporters.

Protecting Declining Industries in the EC

There is a risk, as is always the case when there is a highly active interest and, on the other hand, not very strong interest, that those who have the more active interest will prevail. That risk is undoubtedly great in view of the fact that the European Community has to some extent become the organisation which all members use in order to protect their declining industries. In an odd way it is an organisation for declining rather than rising industries. I do not know how that happened, but it did so at a fairly early date. In the case of agriculture, this is obvious, but it is interesting also that the oldest Community, the Coal and Steel Community, which was set up at the time to promote what most people regarded as the basic industries that would guarantee economic progress, has, with the decline of the coal and steel industries, turned into a protective mechanism too. It is much more concerned with keeping businesses going that should not perhaps be allowed to do so than with stimulating new developments and offering incentives for progress.

The record of the European Community on textiles and international arrangements in that sector is not particularly good. Indeed, the European Community has a good institutional machinery for protecting those who are on the decline and that machinery may well be at the disposal of those whom I mentioned earlier who are interested in the protection of areas that until recently were thought of as being 'hi-tech' and therefore at the frontier of economic development, but which turn out to feel under pressure at this point.

The first question then is: Who will set the tone and determine the momentum of the Community? What will happen about the apparent tradition of the European Community as a protective rather than open organisation?

5

The Definition of Europe

My second question, which from my point of view is the most important at present, is: How do we define Europe? It is hard to exaggerate the importance of this question. It is unfortunate that we increasingly use the words European Community and Europe as if they were synonymous and thereby make statements about Europe that are translated by those who take action into statements about the European Community. While such statements may be correct about Europe they are not so when applied to the European Community. This is particularly evident at present in the relations between the Community and the remaining European Free Trade Association (EFTA) countries. The way in which that relationship is worked out will be the test for the kind of Europe that emerges. Either we find a way of giving the natural partners of the member-states of the European Community in Europe all the advantages of free trade without making them pay a political price for it or we shall document by our attitude to the remaining EFTA countries that we propose to use the European Community to draw boundaries rather than bring down barriers.

The present position is complicated. I confess that I was sceptical when President Delors first made his statement according to which it would be desirable to have bloc-to-bloc negotiations between the European Community and the EFTA countries. It sounded, *mutatis mutandis*, like the familiar statements on the debt problem in Latin America where people say that bloc-to-bloc negotiations are needed between the rich and the poor or the creditors and debtors. That has never made sense nor has it helped anyone who was in a position of indebtedness. It has been a political point that has emphasised differences rather than being productive in any practical way.

It appeared for a day or two after the recent Oslo declaration of the EFTA countries as if Delors's programme might work. It is now clear that that declaration is not worth the paper it was written on and that there is no common position of the remaining EFTA countries. How can there be? There certainly is no common political position and the curious question of whether some of the EFTA countries could pay for free trade by putting money into the coffers of the European Community in exchange for commercial advantages is bound to divide rather than unite them. Austria will continue, for political reasons, to discuss full membership seriously and may perhaps make an application. Switzerland will never apply for membership of the European

Community, not just because of the understanding of neutrality in the Swiss tradition. There are serious differences between Norway and Sweden, and Finland is in a peculiarly difficult position.

The bloc-to-bloc idea does not therefore make sense. We shall have to think again about relations with these countries in a way that can lead beyond reciprocity to a genuine freedom of trade. I confess that in this respect I am a sceptic. I do not like the term 'Fortress Europe'— perhaps fortress is the wrong word—but I suspect that in the first instance there will be a strong tendency within the European Community to define boundaries rather than apply its own internal principles of openness to relations with the outside world. What is done in Europe will, *a fortiori*, be done in the rest of the world.

1992 in a Global Context

My third question—I am more interested in putting the questions before you than answers—is what kind of world will we be living in in relation to 1992, but not only in 1992? Language, here as in other respects, has its own self-fulfilling capacity. More and more people talk about three great blocs in the world. If you look at that language closely it does not make much sense, and yet there are indications that the three economic power centres are giving more substance to their huge regions. North America has a trade agreement between the United States and Canada which may be in the economic interests of Canada, but which for the United States must surely be of political interest in the widest sense. In the Far East we notice above all Japanese investment in the United States and Europe in preparation for 1992. We do not talk so much about the massive investment of Japan in Asia, particularly in South East Asia, although this is one of the important developments of the time. While Japanese investment is not necessarily popular, it is real, and while I am not one of those who believes that the yen will dominate the world, there is no question that Japan is capable of turning many countries in its own orbit into semi-satellites. Indeed, one of the unfortunate side-effects of this three-bloc development is that countries become satellites of larger blocs. They have to adopt the rules of the larger countries and are dependent upon them. That is one of the worst worries about the EFTA countries in Europe.

This is happening at a time when Eastern Europe is opening up. It now looks as if Gorbachev's reforms, certainly with respect to economic development, are likely to fail in the huge Russian empire,

7

but that there may be lasting effects of what has happened in the past few years at the fringes of the empire and certainly in countries such as Poland and Hungary, and probably in the Baltic States, although it remains to be seen how far that will go. It is a bad time to be thinking of three blocs rather than multilateral or international arrangements. This is another challenge to the relative narrowness of much of our thinking.

The Future of Europe?

My fourth and final question is: Where does Europe go from here? These are all big questions and I can therefore be brief, rather than talk all day! It is a curious fact—perhaps borrowed from German history—that the European Community uses trade and trade barriers to define itself in the widest sense politically. Underneath that there are still people who have the curiously mechanical Cartesian—some people call it functionalist—view that if one begins at one corner, such as trade, one is bound to end up with political union and with the United States of Europe. I remember the time when people argued that if you wanted a common market something had to be done about the areas where there was no market nationally, but a national policy, like agriculture. You cannot have a common market, you have to have a common policy. If you have a common policy in one area, such as agriculture, you must have common prices. If you have common prices and then adjust currencies you need to have something like the beginning of a common currency. If you have the beginnings of a common currency, you are bound to have not only a central bank, but common economic policies. If you have a central bank and common economic policies, you are bound to have a common, joint government—and thus the United States of Europe are totally inevitable, once you have decided to begin with the common market.

It is useful to remind oneself that history does not work that way and that we are considering processes which could stop at any point in the chain, and be reversed or taken in different directions. The German example of moving from the *Zollverein* to a unified country is not one of great success even if in some respects the economic success of Germany before 1914 is undeniable.

I have grave doubts that any automaticity will lead from the single market to some of the other objectives which have been mentioned. In particular, I came away from Brussels a sceptic after the 1971 experience of economic and monetary union. There is nothing automatic about it and there is not the slightest reason to believe that a customs union implies monetary union nor that this will necessarily be the next step. If I were to use shorthand, I would say that on European monetary union I am a Sam Brittan sceptic. I am not against the idea of creating an element of stability in a world that is not likely to return to rules of the game that provide stability multilaterally in the near future. It is a complicated process. It does not imply a central bank in the strict sense in which we use the term. It will probably be a process of close co-operation rather than organisation or integration for a long time to come. When we read the Delors Report and its small print we shall see that there is nothing in it to suggest that in the next five to 10 years—or any realistic time-span—the next step will be taken.

'The Habit of Co-operation'

What is happening in the fields of money, foreign policy and, to some extent, even defence policy, is the kind of European co-operation that I have preferred for a long time. The easiest way to describe it is by reminding you of the late Andrew Shonfield's Reith Lectures on 'Europe—Journey to an Unknown Destination'. He said then that for some considerable period, the most important single thing to develop in Europe was what he called the habit of co-operation. The habit of co-operation should not be underestimated; much has happened effectively in that respect in recent years. Central bank governors no longer find it so difficult to talk over the phone to each other or arrange a meeting on Saturday morning in Basle. The same is true of Ministers and senior civil servants and of the whole field of European political co-operation. It is true of ambassadors of the member-states of the Community in other parts of the world.

This habit of co-operation is not strictly institutional. If anyone chose to leave the co-operative system they could, but the habit of co-operation impresses upon people the advantages of keeping each other informed and trying to co-ordinate policies. It may have something to do with the fact that economic policies, as well as certain areas of foreign policy, show more community today than they did in the earlier phases of European Community.

I look forward to seeing a single market that is open to the outside world which contributes to international developments towards free trade and a European system of co-operation that is based as much on habit as on institutions. Let us, then, return to the question 10 years hence to see what the most plausible next steps would be.

2

1992 AND THE BRUSSELS MACHINE

Sir John Hoskyns
Director General,
Institute of Directors,
1984-89

I WILL CONFINE my remarks to the impact of EC developments on British business and the framework required by business to maximise its competitive position. I will digress slightly from this brief in order to move the debate forward, following my speech to the IOD Annual Convention on 28 February 1989.

The Importance of Anecdotal Evidence

First, however, I would like to say something on a more general subject, which is very pertinent to the 1992 debate, that is, the importance of anecdotal evidence. The word 'anecdotal' tends to be used by politicians and civil servants in a pejorative sense, because they confuse two quite different things—evidence in the legal sense and evidence used for making a business judgement. Hearsay evidence in law has no value. But in business and the conduct of affairs, it is often the most valuable evidence of all, because it is *early*. It is the anecdotes, the casual remarks made by people who are not at senior levels, which often provide the first early warnings of potential triumph or disaster in a business. Hence the phrase 'management by walking about', which Commissioners in Brussels may have little time to do. That early information may never be available from all the financial reports or the carefully prepared top management flip-chart presentations.

A single anecdote will have little value. But if there are enough of them, if they come from reliable sources, and if they all point in a particular direction, then the antennae of the astute executive should start to twitch. If the culture or organisational structure is wrong, of course, there may be no one with sufficiently sensitive antennae. Or there may be no one who, when his antennae start to twitch, feels personally responsible for doing something.

There are organisations in which large numbers of intelligent people all know that something is going wrong. But, because they have no vested interest in exposing the problem or because none of them takes seriously the responsibilities of a leadership position, they all just gossip amongst themselves and hope that 'someone up there' knows what is happening—or doesn't know, as the case may be.

When warnings from below (assuming that management style and vested interests allow) are met with repeated requests for hard evidence or statistics, it is likely that someone 'up there' is either naïve about the art of judgement, or is frightened of taking action. Nothing could be more foolish than to deride hunches or intuitive feelings, whether about success or failure. The hunch comes first, the hard evidence later, not the other way round. As in scientific discovery, it is the hunch that triggers the search for the hard evidence which will either refute or confirm it. There are none so blind as those who will not see the writing on the wall, and who instead keep asking for 'proof'. The real world is not like that. I will come back to the question of anecdotes in a moment.

The Institute of Directors totally supports the objectives of the Single Market and Lord Young's 1992 awareness programme, which we believe has been extremely effective. If the IOD view I put forward in early 1989 does nothing else, it should have increased awareness of 1992 even further. If it discourages business men and women in their preparations, they must be a pretty feeble lot. The many letters I have received tell the opposite story. They *want* a Europe without frontiers; they are becoming increasingly doubtful about whether they are going to get it; and they are glad that the IEA, the IOD and others are asking pertinent questions.

1992 'Is Going to Fail'

We believe that, on present indications, 1992 is going to fail, for three reasons. First, insufficient progress is being made on the really difficult measures needed to remove internal frontiers. Second, a great deal of political energy and administrative time is being wasted in drafting vague proposals about European monetary union and trans-European social policies which, even if they are workable and desirable, are not prerequisites for the single market. Third, we believe that the machinery of the Commission and its institutions is organisationally and managerially inadequate for the task facing them.

This is not to say that there are not extremely capable people working with great dedication. There are always such people working on great projects which nevertheless fail—whether in the public or the business sector. We believe that the Brussels bureaucracy may be too small, not too big. We think it lacks the necessary clarity of purpose and management skills, and is set in the wrong organisational structure.

The politicians have rightly been warning business—no doubt in all the member-states—that they are not preparing with sufficient urgency for 1992 and that the increased competitiveness of the single market threatens to wipe them out. Business leaders have not responded with outrage or gone into a sulk about that. They have recognised that it is probably true and are now buckling down to making their preparations. All we are now saying is this: 'You've told us that business must wake up if it is going to be ready for 1992. May we now ask whether 1992 is going to be ready for business?' To our surprise, this question has been received in Brussels with outraged disbelief. How dare we, mere citizens of Europe, question the competence, let alone the probity, of the new European pro-consuls?

This response tells us something about the arrogance or else the insecurity of some people in the Brussels machine; it is on the adequacy of that machine that I would like to focus.

Evidence of Corruption, Fraud and Dishonesty

In fairness to Brussels, however, I do recognise that it was my references to corruption, fraud and dishonesty which understandably provoked them. The four sentences which included those words occupied 12 lines in a text of approximately 300 lines. Just to clear our minds, I would like to read those 12 lines to you. First, on the Community as a whole, I said:

> '[By 1987] there was growing evidence of confused objectives, protectionism, cynical disregard of Community rules, dreams of sixties-style social engineering, administrative incompetence, bureaucratic dishonesty and fraud.

'And there is now, of course, evidence of massive fraud deeply embedded in the Common Agricultural Policy.

'The Single Market project itself is going wrong for all the reasons familiar to most of us in business: shifting objectives, bad organisation, wrong people, poor motivation, inadequate methods, weak management, personal politics—and pilfering on a heroic scale.'

On the Commission itself, I said: 'There are signs that the Brussels machine is becoming corrupted both intellectually and financially.'

I find it strange that, in the light of these remarks, Mr Delors—an experienced *homme d'affaires* who was Finance Minister in the economically disastrous early years of President Mitterrand's first term—should threaten me with legal action. Can you imagine the Chairman of the Stock Exchange making similar threats against anyone who had written or spoken about the worrying evidence of corruption in the City?

When I talked about bureaucratic corruption or dishonesty I was referring primarily to the 'Yes Minister' type of deception, which occurs to a greater or lesser extent in any large bureaucracy (in both the public and private sectors). Indeed, I spelled out one example in detail, where the officials servicing the Economic & Social Committee in Brussels inserted an introduction drafted by themselves, in line with their own preference for tax alignment, into a report containing the opinion of the Economic & Social Committee which was arguing in precisely the opposite direction: an extraordinary episode, which has not been refuted since my speech.

But of course there are other, more uncomfortable, examples. The European Court of Auditors has recently commented on the extraordinarily high proportion of Commission employees reaching the age of 64 who then receive the more advantageous disability pensions instead of normal retirement pensions. The figure, in one category of clerical worker, was, as I understand it, about 40 per cent as compared with about 3 per cent—a percentage which was regarded as actuarially more normal—in a French commercial bank.

At the level of anecdote, what is one to make of the MEP who boasts of having made £100,000 on his expenses in the past four years? When a businessman who has lived in Brussels for years told me about that I was incredulous. But he replied that, judging from other similar boasts he had heard, he reckoned that particular individual was something of an under-achiever. In view of recent uproar, I suppose I should assure Lord Plumb that I am not accusing every MEP of fiddling their expenses. But such reports are in circulation.

How do you translate the term used by the cleaners in the Berlaymont building—'a two overcoat man'? Easy; it means an official who leaves one overcoat on the hook in his office, to show that he's somewhere in the building, while he wears the other on his own business affairs about the city. Perhaps it's all smoke without fire, but we all know what can happen in apparently well-run businesses, if management is not alert, lacks the courage to act promptly, or gradually becomes corrupted itself.

The good salaries and low taxes for Commission employees are not excessive in themselves. The danger is that, because they compare so favourably with those in many—though not the richest—of the member-states, it may be difficult for employees, once habituated to them, to criticise or accept criticism of the organisation which pays them. And it may be just that bit more difficult to expose 'irregularities', to use the popular euphemism.

The Effects of Corruption

Dishonesty, if it exists, does not invalidate the objectives of 1992, nor does it necessarily indicate likely failure of implementation. But my business experience tells me that, once an organisation's culture is corrupted, that organisation is in serious trouble. The infection spreads in the form of cynicism and low morale, lack of commitment to the organisation's goals, and management cowardice leading to lack of mutual trust and self-respect.

Accuracy is essential in this important debate, and I would like to clear up one recent misunderstanding. *The Economist*[1] reported me as saying that the hard details of dismantling frontiers should emerge as a result of 'convergence' following 1992, and dismissed such an idea as unworkable. In fact, the IOD has never made such a suggestion. *The Economist* had misread a part of my speech which referred to European monetary union via 'convergence'. I made it quite clear that barriers could only be removed by measures drawn up and imposed by Brussels, and criticised the Commission for lack of progress on the more difficult measures required.

---

[1] 'Diatribal Rites', *Economist*, 4 March 1989, pp. 18-19.

The Impact of the Single Market on Business

I would now like to say a word about the impact of the single market on business. First, the criterion for success of the single market is very clear and simple. When it is as easy for goods, services, capital and people to move between member-states as it now is within them, we will know that the single market has arrived. For business purposes, the obvious remaining difference will then be that of national currencies. It is quite likely that a parallel currency—probably the European Currency Unit (ECU)—will emerge as, in effect, a single currency. But it is worth remembering that it took 100 years for the dollar to emerge as the single currency in the United States.

Incidentally, we should not lose sight of the 'quality of life' aspects of the single market. Many of us have, I suspect, envied the Americans' freedom of movement—for work, residence and holidays—within their enormous and varied continent. The size and choice may not be quite so spectacular for the post-1992 European, but it will still be an enormous advantage. The real barrier will be language.

Overcoming the Language Barrier

I think it may well come about, therefore, once the whole of the Community is as accessible for business as the United Kingdom is for us today, that the mastery of language will turn out to be the key strategic preparation. It may be that, with hindsight, we will realise that the answer to that difficult question which has been plaguing many businessmen and women over the last two years, 'Yes, but what do we actually *do* in our company to prepare for 1992?', is that they should have developed a language capability, at least covering the other three of the big four (France, Germany and Italy), as the first step. Once that has been done, a company can start familiarising itself with the business culture in other member-states and building up individual business contacts there. Even within the member-states, cultures and temperaments vary. Many people will argue that doing business in Hamburg is totally different from doing business in Munich.

The fact that English is the common business language in the Community is almost certainly a disadvantage for us. Businessmen and women in the other member-states only need to learn English—the new Esperanto—in order to be able to communicate on equal terms with most of their counterparts in the other European countries and on more than equal terms in the UK.

I suspect that the UK is thus at a unique disadvantage, rather than an advantage, unless it becomes better than its partners in languages. And we all know that it is at present a great deal worse. I say that with all humility, being a classic non-linguist myself, and spoilt by being married to a half-foreign wife who speaks French passably and Italian fluently, and with a brother-in-law who adds fluent German and Spanish as well.

'The Brussels Machine'

Now, a look at the Brussels machine. The recent House of Lords Select Committee Report on fraud against the Community provides some valuable insights.[2] I am told that it is unusual for such reports to be accompanied by a press release. And the release itself—presumably drafted by civil servants—is rather misleading. It puts much more emphasis on their Lordships' criticism of the member-state governments than on their criticism of Brussels. Unfortunately, it is of course this release, rather than the report itself, which is reflected in the rather subdued press comment, most of which suggested that the main culprits are the Community partners rather than the Commission.

I doubt if their Lordships saw the press release in draft, so my antennae twitch a little. Let me therefore try to correct that no doubt unintended bias, because the House of Lords Report does tell us a lot about the unworkability of the Commission's present arrangements and the failure of the machine to grapple with the difficulties, and therefore about the efficiency of the machine itself.

More anecdotal evidence

First, however, it is time for some more anecdotes which are I think relevant to our judgement of the adequacy of that machine. Let us start with the ridiculous and move on to the serious. Apparently there was recently a debate in the European Parliament about genetic engineering and 'test tube' babies. The debate ended in confusion when the German reference to 'frozen semen' was translated into Danish as 'very cold sailors'. Then there was the proposal that a liberal supply of condoms should be provided for offshore fishermen going off on trips of more than 48 hours. As one of the skippers said, 'They must think we are a pretty funny lot'.

---

[2] House of Lords Select Committee on the European Communities, Session 1988-89, 5th Report: *Fraud Against the Community—With Evidence*, HL Paper 27, London: HMSO, 1989.

One of my people spent a day attending a meeting of the Economic & Social Committee last year and listened to a one-and-a-half-hour debate on whether the word 'substantial' was the *mot juste* for inclusion in a draft opinion. There is the true story of the Brussels official who was sailing on holiday in the Baltic when a piece of equipment broke on his yacht. To his fury, he found that he could not get a replacement in the local marina. Immediately on his return from holiday he drafted a directive laying down that all yacht fittings should be standardised in all 12 Community countries. Of course, such proposals never see the light of day, but they tell us something about the cast of mind of those who, if they are not careful, begin to think that they are Europe's masters rather than its servants.

More seriously, I referred earlier to the contradictory introduction provided by officials to an opinion of the Economic & Social Committee. A Foreign Office official who read the transcript of my Convention speech told me that this was a meaningless example because some parts of the Commission do not take the Economic & Social Committee seriously and would like to close it down. The same sentiment was expressed to me by an ex-Brussels Commissioner sitting next to me at a conference I attended in Germany three years ago.

I hope the 189 members of the Economic & Social Committee, who flog out to Brussels for two or three days most weeks, for no pay, out-of-pocket expenses only (and who are charged higher prices in the Brussels canteen than are charged to their permanent officials), are not upset by that.

But the question remains. *Should* the Commission take EcoSoc seriously? If not, would it be better to close down the Committee and save its annual servicing budget of about £30 million a year? After all, it is only a collection of ordinary citizens representing employers, trade unions, professionals, academics and consumers. Or is the truth rather different? Do some Community officials rubbish EcoSoc simply because it dares to criticise them?

One last example: the European Court of Auditors recently reported that the 1987 Brussels financial year for farm spending has been arbitrarily cut from 12 to 10 months by the Commission in order to give the impression that spending had risen by only 3·6 per cent (in line with the Council of Ministers' Fontainebleau Agreement) when the actual increase was more like 25 per cent. In business, people get fired for that sort of thing.

The Extent of Fraud in the CAP

The House of Lords Select Committee Report addresses the problems of the widespread fraud and irregularities committed against the funds which the Economic Community raises and disburses, in the relatively few areas in which it plays a direct financial role. This means, for the most part, at present, the financial labyrinths of the Common Agricultural Policy (CAP)—levies, export subsidies, storage payments and Monetary Compensatory Amounts.

The report is cagey about the extent of fraud (which, by its nature is hard to estimate), but does not dismiss the figures of between £2 billion and £6 billion per annum suggested by an expert witness. As the Economic Community's total income for 1987 was about £25 billion, these figures should give considerable cause for concern.

The reasons for this highly unsatisfactory state of affairs are partly structural, partly attitudinal, and partly managerial, and cast severe doubts on the ability of the existing institutions to manage the Community effectively.

The constitutional and administrative structure of the Community is a buck-passer's and paper-pusher's dream. Responsibilities are shared between the Commission and its administrative back-up, the Council of Ministers and member-states' government and parliamentary machines, and the European Parliament, in such a way that no direct chain of accountability can be established. Everyone can blame someone else when something goes wrong.

In the agricultural sphere it is the Council that decides the level of payments; the Commission that is responsible for devising the administrative system to determine eligibility and budgeting, subject to some control by the Parliament; and the member-states who are responsible for paying them, accounting for them, and ensuring that they are paid to the right people for the right reasons. This is not a recipe for effective financial control.

Tensions between Eurocrats and National Governments

At the attitudinal level there is a constant tension between the professional Europeans—not necessarily just the Commission and its staff—who want to build up the powers and functions of the central institutions; and the corresponding interests in member-states, who wish to take advantage of whatever the Community has to offer, but do not want to lose control of their national power base.

One result of this tension is the over-elaboration of administrative practices when the centralisers get their foot in the door. As an example, the Common Customs Tariff created by the Commission, which determines import levies on agricultural products, contains 4,000 product codes for agricultural products alone, 932 more codes for processed foods, 1,416 standard recipes and 14,000 non-standard recipes. It is so precise that it can permit different levies to be paid on different kinds of biscuits depending on their fat, sugar and flour contents.

Another result is that member-states will stand on their dignity if they are requested to give Community officials powers to operate independently on their hitherto sovereign territory. Moreover, since there is little co-ordination between criminal codes, it would be extremely difficult for Community officials to acquire expertise in each of the member-states' enforcement procedures.

It was quite easy for the Commission, in its first response to the House of Lords report, to blame member-states for not giving it adequate powers, and to point out that enforcement procedures were largely in the hands of member-states' governments. This is true, as far as it goes, but the report contains plenty of examples of the Commission failing to give adequate guidance on the regulations which the member-states have to apply. That is managerial failing.

Member-states are supposed to report 'irregularities' in CAP disbursements. But there is no definition of 'irregularity'. Perhaps it is more difficult to define than a biscuit. The Commission has no up-to-date rules about checking procedures to be used by member-states, and no systematic analysis is made of any reports that are received. A compendium of reported irregularities was last revised in 1980.

At a higher level, the Community's Court of Auditors, which provides an independent audit facility for the Community, was established only in 1977 (20 years after the Treaty of Rome was signed). It still has insufficient staff to provide anything like a full audit coverage and suffers from considerable internal differences of opinion about the true function of public-sector audit. There is no formal mechanism for ensuring that its report on the Community's annual accounts is taken into consideration in the elaborate procedures which are undertaken by the Parliament and the Council of Ministers to approve the Community's accounts and give the Commission its 'discharge' for the financial year. Only in 1988 did the Commission set up a (completely inadequate) 'Anti-fraud Co-ordination Unit' to perform an integrated internal audit function in this area.

Financial Control Unsatisfactory

So far, not a very satisfactory picture. If this is the best it can achieve in managing the limited executive functions that it now performs, it is just as well that the Community has so few functions which actually require it to do something as opposed to simply thinking about it. Financial control is, after all, the most basic—and in some ways the most straightforward—function of management.

But the 1992 initiative, as a whole, is a project which needs the most careful managing. Much of the work will entail badgering member-states' governments to do things about which they may, at best, feel lukewarm. This is not so much now a matter of getting the Council of Ministers to pass directives—though many of the most difficult still remain to be passed. It is more a matter of getting them implemented once they are passed.

To remove border controls by 1992—which is what the member-states committed themselves to when they signed the Single European Act—requires a huge legislative and administrative effort in every member-state. New systems have to be devised to collect taxes, to maintain animal and plant health, to prevent the import of terrorists, drugs, firearms, anglers' lead weights, and all the other things which at present get stopped at the border. This will need constant progress-chasing to ensure implementation, and constant monitoring to prevent backsliding thereafter.

In reviewing the progress of the single market programme, the Institute of Directors has suggested that three things should be examined: the objectives, in order to remove the present confusion between essential and non-essential or even damaging measures; the progress to date in achieving the former; and the adequacy of the Brussels machine—my subject for today. On present evidence which, in the light of the House of Lords report, is getting steadily less anecdotal as the days pass, I believe that the Brussels machine is simply not up to the job.

3

THREE MODELS OF EUROPEAN INTEGRATION

Victoria Curzon Price

Professor of Economics, Institut Universitaire d'Etudes Européennes,
University of Geneva,
and Visiting Faculty Member,
International Management Institute, Geneva

EUROPE SINCE the Second World War has been a veritable testing ground for different institutional methods of achieving integration, both economic and political. In fact, the story of European integration to date is a good example of the Hayekian thesis that it is not only the economy that proceeds by trial and error, but that the same principle applies to the unconscious formation of other institutions, such as parliaments, courts or even the language we use to communicate with each other.

For the first 35 years after the end of the War we had two distinct models of integration to study and criticise: the Common Market (comprising the European Economic Community, EURATOM and the European Coal and Steel Community), on the one hand, and the European Free Trade Association (EFTA), on the other. Since 1985 we have had a third model—the *Single* Market. At the risk of over-simplification, one could say that if the Common Market represented a steam-roller approach to integration, EFTA was more of a light-weight Mini. Neither model was ideal, so it was only a matter of time before a new one was introduced. This happened in 1985-86 with the adoption of the Single Market project and the amendments to the Treaty of Rome contained in the Single Act, by which the 12 member-states may well have taken an option on a Ferrari. Whether they are actually up to driving it remains to be seen—but the model itself is very fast, very expensive and very original.

The 'Mini' Model

EFTA always represented the minimalist approach to integration. Only *economic* integration was actually aimed at. In fact, one of the main theses which EFTA was meant to demonstrate was the idea that economic and political integration could be divorced from one another, that economic integration did not necessarily lead to political integration, and that economic integration needed only the very lightest of institutional structures.

More fundamentally, EFTA was based on two essential federalist principles, namely, the principle of subsidiarity, on the one hand, and a respect for other people's differences, on the other. The theory of federalism is not something with which people who live in a unitary state are necessarily very familiar, and indeed I have noticed that the term 'federalism' is used in a very different sense in Great Britain and on the Continent. In the UK 'federalism' is a nasty bogeyman, based in Brussels and threatening British sovereignty, while elsewhere it is simply a sensible way of reconciling a minimum of unity with a maximum of diversity. The way federalism does this is, firstly, to apply the principle of subsidiarity to all problems that arise: *never allow a higher-level institutional body to undertake a task that a lower-level body could accomplish just as well.* This implies a systems-approach to the division of social tasks: the family, the local community, the town, the province (canton, länder), the country, the international organisation form a set of hierarchic and concentric circles (the highest level being at the centre), each one best adapted to solve particular sets of problems. Federalism emphasises the need to keep the centre weak and the periphery strong and implies a belief in the ability of lower-level institutions to solve most problems—otherwise it would not be able to accommodate diversity.

This brings us to the second element of federalism relevant to the EFTA model: the whole point of federations being to allow different communities to live together peacefully, they have to tolerate differences. This means not just putting up with other people's funny ways, but also not trying to impose one's own funny ways on others. No sub-unit within a federation may attempt to dominate another, or that would be the end of the federation ...

A broad framework of free trade—integration via the market

EFTA was based on the conviction that all one needed was a broad framework (free trade between member-states) and one could then leave the actual task of *integration* (namely, specialisation and trade) to the market. This was the subsidiarity principle at work: integration was left to a low-level, non-political institution. Within this framework there was certainly no need for common policies, for instance in social, regional, or monetary affairs, and no need for harmonisation of laws. It was assumed that the market could handle the task of integration, that trade thrived on the basis of differences—and anyway, were we not trying to prove that economic integration could be kept clear of entangling political commitments?

The conviction that free trade could cope with virtually any amount of diversity even went as far as the idea that each member-state could retain its own tariff policy. And although origin rules blunted the effect of the potential distortions due to diversity in trade policy, they were so lenient that in practice high tariffs lost their economic effect through direct and indirect trade deflections—a technical point which I will not expand on here, but which serves merely to underscore the extent to which EFTA countries were prepared to allow trade to develop on an untidy, unharmonised basis.

The fact that agriculture was not included is significant. It was the one sector in the economies of the EFTA countries where market forces had long since been replaced by government ones in determining prices and levels of output. Such a sector could not be exposed to free trade, for otherwise, different member-states' agricultural policies would have been put into competition with one another. This was *not* the purpose of the exercise! Alternatively, a *common* agricultural policy could have been agreed upon, à la CAP, but this did not fit the 'Mini/federalist' model, so agriculture was simply left out—and one lived with the differences that were thus implied.

Wide price differences and distortions—EFTA diversity

Yet the implications of *not* agreeing to uniform farm prices, of *not* establishing a common external tariff, of *not* attempting any institutional harmonisation at all, meant that the industrialists who were supposed to be doing the actual job of integration had to accept the wide range of price differences *and* distortions (a sort of economic 'noise') emanating from the very different institutional set-ups which co-existed within the Association. Indeed, the EFTA of the 1960s could hardly have included a more variegated group of countries. One could find both large and small, developed and under-developed, socialist and conservative, high-tax and low-tax, the welfare-state minded and the self-help enthusiasts, interventionists and non-interventionists, neutrals and members of NATO—and the list could easily be extended. The only thing which united them at the time was their shared dislike of the 'steam-roller' model of integration on offer from the European Community—and perhaps a desire to demonstrate that their Mini could actually work and achieve its limited objectives.

They were lucky on both counts. The sorting-out process whereby some members shifted camps helped to make EFTA slightly less diverse (and the EC rather more so). As the Association lost members, so its sheer importance in terms of import and export shares for each of its members diminished. Geographically it remained almost as dispersed as ever. All of which meant that trade based on intra-area diversity was unlikely to give rise to insoluble problems—and it in fact did not. More significantly, however, the 'Mini' model was used to forge the economically vital bilateral links between the EC and the members of EFTA, some of whom were more dependent on the EC than many EC members were themselves. Origin rules were tightened up (tolerance of diversity was not a well-developed EC principle), but otherwise the 'Mini' model was adopted without modification. After 15 years of operation without serious hitches one can only conclude that it is tough, reliable and inexpensive in terms of loss of sovereignty. But of course it does not take you very far ...

The 'Steam-Roller' Model

The 'steam-roller' model was very different. Although the political aspects of the Treaty of Rome were well disguised, there is no denying that there was more afoot than mere economic integration. The elaborate institutions, the famous three stages culminating in the principle of qualified majority voting, the absence of a withdrawal clause, the very *scope* of the enterprise—free movement of goods, services, people and capital, not to speak of numerous 'common policies'—were truly breath-taking. The contrast to the light-weight Mini could not be more striking. In fact, the Treaties of Rome and Paris had to be strong, for they were supposed to be carrying forward the hope of European unity. In particular, they were the concrete emanation of the *functionalist theory* of European unification.

The functionalist approach, of which Robert Schumann and Jean

Monnet were keen and politically effective proponents, started from the premise that nation states had to be deprived of their sovereignty gradually and by stealth, for they would never part with it willingly. This could be accomplished by proceeding in small *functional* steps: if sovereign states could be persuaded to co-operate with one another over a trivial technical issue (like harmonising road signs), or if they could be made to see the wisdom of pooling resources in a particular economic sector (like coal and steel), and *if* they agreed to let these technical, sectoral matters be managed from the centre by a semi-independent authority, then all one needed to do was gradually to build up a portfolio of such agreements. Nation states would get used to the idea of co-operating with each other and, as time went by, one could attempt more and more ambitious projects. One day the nation state would be caught, like Gulliver, by hundreds of sovereignty-stripping agreements.

The essence of the strategy, according to Monnet, was to stick to technical, functional matters as much as possible, for technicians from different countries would generally be able to agree on a technical solution to a problem, while politicians could be relied upon to make a mess of things. However, as their appetite for complicated technical dossiers was known to be limited, there was every chance that the experts would be left a free hand to 'build Europe' ...

The functionalist fantasy: centralism and the CAP

It goes without saying that the nation state was not taken in for a single minute and in 1965 General de Gaulle, pouring scorn on *'les technocrates apatrides de Bruxelles'*, put a stop to decision-making by qualified majority vote. Though deprived of this essential corner-stone in the functionalists' decision-making process, the European Community nevertheless had to live out the functionalist fantasy in practice—its institutions, its scope, its philosophy reflected this amazing centralising principle: anything which could conceivably be managed from the centre should be, as it would somehow be existential proof that national sovereignty was withering away.

The Common Agricultural Policy (CAP) is a particularly good example of functionalism at work. Forging a single agricultural policy out of several national ones, to be managed from the centre by a semi-independent Commission, was politically a very difficult and ambitious task, requiring a fair transfer of sovereignty from member-states. And what a monument to integration it became! For many years the CAP was *the* symbol of European integration. The longer the marathon negotiating sessions took, the more often the clock was stopped to meet a self-imposed deadline, the more exhausted the Ministers of Agriculture at the end of the annual price-fixing ceremony, the more delighted we were supposed to be. No matter that the actual content of the agreement was economic nonsense—*this* was integration.

And what integration! The price of wheat was fixed at a level common to all, then the forces of free trade were unleashed. When exchange-rate movements threatened the uniform price structure, encouraging French farmers to expand at the expense of the German, 'green' currencies were introduced, accompanied by 'monetary compensation amounts'. Only then could market forces be unleashed again.

Harmonisation of prices—'a travesty of integration'

Needless to say, this was a travesty of what integration, whether political or economic, was really about. Economic integration, it is true, is supposed to produce uniform prices (according to the one-market, one-price theorem), but only as *an end-result of a process*, in which competition, fuelled by price *differences*, plays the lead role, forcing entrepreneurs to seek out areas of comparative advantage, specialise and reap the gains from trade, more efficient scale of production, and so forth. If prices are made uniform by a complex bureaucratic-political process as a *starting point*, then competition disappears, there is no reason to trade, reallocate resources or specialise. The harmonisation of prices as a starting point is, in reality, an absolute travesty of integration—yet it looks the same to the untrained eye. From the point of view of political integration it is meaningless too, since it implies agreement according to the lowest common denominator (in this case, the highest acceptable price).

Other examples of functionalism at work included the European Coal and Steel Community, at one time into five-year plans and uniform prices generated from a complex basing-point system; Euratom—which never got off the ground because the nation state was not taken in by functionalist theories; the Davignon Steel Plan, which fixed both prices *and* quantities (quite an achievement from a technical point of view); the European Monetary System (EMS—a perfect functionalist institution in that it is so technical hardly anybody understands it, while at the same time it implies a considerable loss of sovereignty); and, of course, the lengthy and exceedingly technical negotiations which went into producing detailed specifications for Euro-cars, Euro-tractors, Euro-jam and so on.

The trouble with the functionalist theory of integration, with which the EC was lumbered, was that it posited *harmonisation as a starting point*, not simply of prices but of all sorts of social, institutional and legal parameters. Only then, it was felt, would free trade in goods, services, capital and labour also be *fair* trade. However, as member-states turned out to be singularly lacking in 'political will' (constantly reduced to zero by the principle of unanimity), the centralism implied in the functionalist philosophy never got very far in practice. All that happened was that free trade and integration simply did not occur. By 1985 non-tariff barriers based on technical and safety specifications had succeeded in fragmenting the so-called Common Market into 12 separate markets; an EC transport policy (provided for in the Treaty of Rome) had not been agreed upon, with the result that road, rail, air and water transport remained thoroughly cartellised; most member-states maintained exchange controls, which meant that the free movement of capital, also provided for in the Treaty of Rome, was out of the question; and the same could be said of the service sector and the free movement of qualified people. In the meantime, the customs union had not jeopardised the jobs of customs officers, who were needed in ever larger numbers to verify the increasingly complex formalities which traded goods needed to comply with—and to collect VAT, which was, of course, just a consumption tax levied at the frontier and not a tariff.

If all these matters had to be resolved between now and 1992 according to the old centralising principle, no one would believe that anything real was going to happen at all . . .

The 'Ferrari' Model

The 'steam-roller' model having proved ineffective, it was replaced in 1985-86 by something quite new. The process by which the new model was designed and introduced will delight Mandevillian students of institutional evolution,[1] because it was to some extent the unintended

---

[1] Bernard Mandeville, a Dutch doctor practising what would nowadays be called psychiatry in London at the end of the seventeenth century, has achieved a place in the history of ideas for his critique of rationalism, suggesting that the consequences of our decisions are often very different from our intentions. He extended this idea to the whole order of society, whose institutions were not deliberately invented

[*Contd. on p. 30*]

result of past actions and in some measure, I remain convinced, of ignorance as to its broader implications, especially those involving loss of government sovereignty. (I make a distinction here between national sovereignty, which involves the right of parliaments to pass laws as they see fit, and government sovereignty, which involves the freedom of governments to act in a discretionary fashion.)

The new model of integration is spelled out in the Commission's 1985 White Paper and is based on the now-famous 1979 ruling of the European Court of Justice (ECJ) in the *Cassis-de-Dijon* case. Here the ECJ tipped the balance in favour of Article 30 of the Treaty of Rome (prohibition of all restrictions on imports) and against Article 36 (providing for exceptional import restrictions 'justified on grounds of public morality, public policy or public security; the protection of health and life of humans, animals or plants'). The view of the Court was that if a product had been 'lawfully produced and marketed' in one member-state, another member-state could invoke Article 36 only if an *overriding* public interest were at stake. In other words, member-states had to recognise the validity of their partners' approach to ensuring the safety of products, unless they could prove to the Court's satisfaction that a particular standard constituted a genuine threat to health, morality, or national security.

The new approach: 'mutual recognition and equivalence'

The implications of this judgement have been long in coming but they were developed and extended in the Commission's 1985 White Paper. Here the Commission announced its 'new approach' to technical (safety, health, environmental) standards:

> 'The general thrust of the Commission's approach in this area will be *to move away from the concept of harmonisation towards that of mutual recognition and equivalence.*'[2]

The beauty of this notion is quite striking. In its purest form, member-states simply recognise that by passing national laws on safety,

---

but 'had grown up by the survival of what proved successful'. See in particular, 'Lecture on a master mind' delivered to the British Academy on 23 March 1966 by F. A. von Hayek and published in *Proceedings of the British Academy*, Vol. LII, London, 1967.

[2] Commission of the European Communities, *Completing the Internal Market: White Paper from the Commission to the European Council*, Brussels: CEC, 1985, p. 6, para. 13.

health, environmental protection and so on, they are all attempting to achieve the same general ends and agree that there are many different and equally valid means of achieving them. The ends are common, but the means can differ.

In principle, the Community has at last broken with its centralising past, according to which a *single* Euro-norm had to be agreed upon before trade could be allowed to flow freely. From now on, according to the 'new approach', member-states need only agree on *'essential requirements'* in broad terms, leaving individual members free to decide on how to satisfy them. The technique used by the Commission is to work through Directives, which leave the method and form of implementation up to individual member-states to decide upon.

Once a product is covered by such a 'Framework Directive' and meets its own country's laws, it is deemed to meet the 'essential requirements' and must be granted the right to free circulation within the Community. If it is felt that a common standard would nevertheless be useful (for instance in standardising telephone-switching equipment), the Commission *no longer attempts to undertake this task itself*, but instead passes it on to non-governmental, industry-based standards-making bodies.

Applying the EFTA federal principles

The two federal principles which lay behind the old EFTA model are in practice being applied here: respect for other countries' differences (mutual recognition), on the one hand, and subsidiarity (handing over to non-governmental standards-making bodies), on the other. Together, they actually make it conceivable that a Single Market might really be created by 1992, since they cut through yards of bureaucratic red-tape at a single stroke.

It is also significant that the principle of mutual recognition can apply to services as well as to goods. Indeed, without this short-cut, the creation of a single market for services in less than four years would hardly be credible. As it is, Framework Directives have been prepared for banking, insurance and audio-visual services, which are in various stages of adoption by the Council; the mutual recognition of professional qualifications is already well advanced, although some guilds are putting up a stout defence; and some progress is even being made in that nest of quotas and restrictions of every description, road transport.

Finally, agreement on Framework Directives has been speeded up by the adoption, in the Single Act, of qualified majority voting. By November 1988, the Council of Ministers had adopted or reached a 'common position' on 108 out of the total of 279 proposals required to abolish internal frontiers by December 1992.[3] The Commission is unhappy with the rate of progress, claiming that the 171 remaining measures must be adopted within the next two years in order to give member-states time to incorporate them into national law before 1 January 1993. In particular, no apparent progress appears to have been made in the area of 'approximation' of VAT rates and coverage, nor in the matter of excise taxes on petrol, drinks and cigarettes, which account for about 30 of the measures which remain to be tabled and/or adopted. As everyone knows, member-states have reserved their veto rights on fiscal matters, so agreement in these areas is likely to be very difficult. It is also unfortunately true that unless agreement is reached on the approximation of VAT and excise taxes, internal frontiers are likely to remain.

Although the break with the recent past is striking (when one was lucky if the Council managed to agree on more than 10 Directives a year), progress is still agonisingly slow and unlikely to speed up, especially if governments insist on 'Framework Directives' for every conceivable sector of industry and services, and dig their toes in over indirect taxation. Will the deadline be met?

Using the Principle of Competing Jurisdictions to Meet the 1992 Deadline

In essence, the principle of mutual recognition puts different regulatory systems into competition with each other, either muffled by 'Framework Directives' or directly. By 1 January 1993, all goods and services will fall into one or the other category: either they are covered by a Framework Directive or they are not; either the Framework Directive has been incorporated into national law, or it has not. At this moment, member-states must have the courage simply to abolish internal EC frontier controls, as they have in principle promised to do.

This will have a galvanising effect on the process of harmonisation, but instead of having to rely on agreement between member-states,

---

[3] Commission of the European Communities, *Completing the Internal Market: an area without internal frontiers. Progress report required by Article 8B of the Treaty*, Com (88) 650, Brussels: CEC, 17 November 1988, p. 4, para. 9.

one can instead rely on governments to adopt the necessary measures spontaneously. This is because free trade on the basis of different regulatory systems puts the regulatory systems themselves into direct competition with each other. There is no reason why they might not simply co-exist, giving consumers a wider range of choice than was previously available, but it is likely that the process of competition will soon establish a ranking, from the 'most preferred' to the 'least preferred' norms. In the latter case, from then on, the ball is in the individual member-state's court. It can either do nothing, thus burdening its local industry with an unpopular norm (off the standard price/quality trade-off curve) and basically condemning it to slow death in the long term, or it can adapt its legislation spontaneously—by far the more likely option.

If it is found that, in the absence of a Framework Directive, competition between jurisdictions is pushing standards to an unacceptably low level, the incentive to agree on 'essential requirements' will be substantial.

But this is not really a problem in areas where the intrinsic quality, safety or durability of the product for the user is at issue (for instance, in defining what is a jam, or what the minimum performance for brakes on cars should be). Here, one should simply rely on the wisdom of the market itself, if properly informed. The eternal trade-off between cost and quality is one that consumers should be allowed to determine. If they signal that they like a low-quality, low-cost product, and thus push standards to an unacceptably low level, one should ask: unacceptable *to whom*? Presumably, unacceptable to those stuck with a high-quality, high-cost norm! But of course that is no argument. In any event, the whole problem is doubtless exaggerated, since the well-informed market is increasingly likely to prefer a high-quality/high-price norm to a low-quality/low-price one, because of rising real incomes.

There is also a lot to be said for leaving legislatures free to experiment in this domain, especially at a time of rapid technological change. If the Community could nerve itself for competing jurisdictions in this area, it would be a jump ahead of other countries, such as the USA or Japan, because it would have a system for experimenting simultaneously with several possible norms in rapidly evolving areas. Once the market selects the optimal norm, countries can be expected to converge on it all by themselves.

Difficulties with environmental standards: negative externalities
Where the principle of competing jurisdictions is likely to cause
problems is in environmental standards. This is because in this matter
one is no longer just considering the intrinsic qualities of the product
for the users, but its negative externalities—its impact on others. But
even here distinctions can be drawn. When negative externalities are
'contained' within the jurisdiction of the country enacting the legislation (in other words, it produces no negative externalities for other
jurisdictions), there is no reason why harmonisation should be
attempted.

For instance, suppose that Germany has very exacting worker-safety
rules in the chemical industry, thus raising production costs as
compared with Portugal or Spain. The chemical products circulating
freely within the Single Market will reflect the different attitudes to the
negative externality (the danger of producing the good). But there is
really no reason why Portugal should be obliged to raise its worker-
safety rules, or Germany to lower hers. These are societal value
judgements to be decided internally, at national level. Each country
should remain free to decide how to allocate national income between
competing objectives—for that is what worker-safety legislation
amounts to. The same goes, incidentally, for social security systems,
direct taxation and the like. All these are basically *consumption*
decisions with no spill-over effects on other countries: How and on
what should the national income be spent? More safety at work? More
education? More defence? There are so many claims! But it would be
most presumptuous to say that they should be harmonised at
Community level.

However, should the negative externality under consideration *not* be
contained within the jurisdiction—and a great deal of pollution has no
respect for jurisdictional boundaries—then it is not enough to say that
each member-state should be left free to determine its own level of
pollution control. In this case, competition between jurisdictions
would be inefficient, just as competition between individuals is
inefficient in the presence of negative externalities. Here international
agreement, for instance prohibiting the use of inert gases that
destroy the earth's ozone layer, is obviously to be preferred to a free-
for-all, where some countries would have strict (hence costly) requirements, and others would have none. Free trade between such
groups of countries would result in more ozone being destroyed more
quickly.

There is another instance where the principle of free trade based on mutual recognition would produce unacceptable results. This is when: (a) the product itself causes undesirable side-effects (e.g. polluting vehicles); (b) these side-effects are considered important by a significant part of the population of one or more member-states; but (c) different member-states attach widely differing values to them.

Under these circumstances a uniform pan-European standard, though doubtless desirable, may not be achievable, while mutual recognition would by the same token prove politically unacceptable. Such cases, it should be emphasised, are likely to be few and far between, for all three conditions mentioned above need to be fulfilled simultaneously (it being up to the courts to dismiss frivolous claims); nor do they constitute a threat to the Single Market concept, since these exceptions can be dealt with by non-frontier measures.

A democratic federal system has to find ways of accommodating such differences. Thus Denmark (like California for that matter) should be allowed to specify stricter anti-pollution requirements for cars *even* if this means prohibiting the importation of Fiats and Renaults and implicitly favouring Mercedes and BMW's. These are politically sensitive value-judgements where minority (Danish) rights have to be respected by the European majority for the federal spirit to survive. Here, the principle of free trade and competing jurisdictions is overridden by a more important consideration: the right to express different societal values within a grouping as vast and diverse as Western Europe—a principle, incidentally, provided for in Article 36 of the Treaty of Rome.

Where competition between jurisdictions *is* likely to push legislation to an unacceptably low level is in the area of taxation—VAT, excise taxes, and withholding tax on interest on savings deposits and bonds— precisely the area where unanimous inter-governmental agreement is going to prove very difficult to obtain. Well, let us free trade and capital movements and see how fast some sort of compromise is hammered out! And if it is not, what is unacceptable to governments will be more than acceptable to tax-payers, who so seldom possess the power to affect their destiny.

In any event, member-states are not even waiting for 1992 to bring their various laws spontaneously into line, so the 'new approach' is already making its presence felt.

The Implications of a Single Market for Capital

In June 1988 member-states agreed, to everyone's astonishment, to abolish exchange controls by July 1990 (with rather longer time-tables for Greece, Spain and Portugal). A free market for capital is, of course, on the Single Market agenda, but it has been a pleasant surprise to see governments actually undertake such a commitment.

It represents an astonishing break with the past. It means that the French, the Italians, the Danes will be free to keep their savings in ECUs, dollars, yen or any Community currency of their choice (the Briton or the German is already free to do so). This means that governments will no longer be able to mask the results of economic mismanagement, which unscrupulous and unpatriotic speculators tend to spot rather quickly, sending—in a free market—the value of the currency down in relation to other, better-managed, currencies. To avoid this daily evaluation of government policies by the market is, after all, the reason why exchange controls were introduced in the first place. Now our governments appear to be prepared to submit to its unyielding discipline. Why? Are they so sure that they can pass the test? Do they welcome this 'outside' discipline as a way of warding off domestic pressure groups? Have they suddenly turned over a new leaf? *For the abolition of exchange controls sharply reduces the scope for discretionary action on the part of government.*

How does one *persuade* (as opposed to compelling) 57 million Italians to save in the national currency? Presumably by offering market rates of interest. This means an end to manipulating interest rates as an instrument of industrial policy, and should certainly dampen collective enthusiasm for running large and expensive fiscal deficits. Both effects constitute a direct challenge to the discretionary powers of governments.

The EMS without exchange control

How does one keep the European Monetary System going without exchange control? It is, after all, not such an amazing performance to keep a currency within agreed price limits if one retains the right to control the quantities coming onto the market. Without such powers, one is reduced to managing one's currency at least as well as the Germans do theirs. This implies competition between monetary and fiscal policies, with the lowest-inflation country setting the pace for all the rest. Again, this is an incredible reduction in the scope for discretionary government action.

It is often said, and rightly so, that creating a single European currency would represent such a loss of sovereignty that were we to get there, we would not be far off full political integration. And yet, if EMS governments stick to their stated commitments—free trade, free movement of capital and fixed exchange rates—they will have tied their hands as firmly as if they had actually created a European central bank: in fact, their policy objectives will have become 'over-determined' and virtually impossible to achieve simultaneously. Even if they retain the right to vary their exchange rates within the EMS, the need to compete for their citizens' savings will force them to behave with extreme fiscal and monetary caution.

Conclusion

We saw at the outset that the functionalist theory of integration presumed to deprive the nation state of sovereignty by stealth—stealing little bits of it until gradually there would be no fight left in the animal. This aspect of the 'steam-roller' model never worked, but what remained was a stifling centralised approach to economic integration and an amazing confusion of ends and means: the centralised policies themselves became evidence of political integration in the making, irrespective of their impact in terms of economic integration.

We also argued that the 'Mini-model' approach to integration claimed to be able to achieve economic integration without any loss of political sovereignty whatsoever by allowing free trade to proceed on the basis of differences, without extensive harmonisation.

While the 'steam-roller' model collapsed under its own weight, the Mini, though successful, was very limited. The full implications of allowing real free trade to develop without harmonisation of technical standards were hidden because there was never any question of abolishing intra-area frontiers, nor of extending the model to other than trade in industrial goods. The Single Market approach, by essentially adopting the Mini model's federalist philosophy (subsidiarity and respect for other peoples' differences), but taking the additional radical step of applying it to goods, services, people and capital, has created an entirely new approach to integration—perhaps rather optimistically called in this essay the 'Ferrari' model.

Whether it actually works this time around or not (and some justified doubts have been raised in this regard) is almost unimportant, in the sense that the model itself is sound. It is available for use by future generations of political leaders if this one fails in its self-appointed task of creating a genuine Single Market in Western Europe by—let us be generous—1995.

The most interesting aspect of the 'Ferrari' model is not even economic. It lies in the process of competing jurisdictions: as governments spontaneously manage their economies better, actively seek optimal regulatory norms and restore whole swathes of decisions to the market, are we not witnessing the sort of self-restraint in economic policy-making that constitutional economists have suggested should be imposed by law? Is this not a simpler, neater, more natural route? It is not that the 'Ferrari model' deprives nation states of their sovereignty, but it does give governments a strong incentive not to mismanage their economies.

4

THE SOCIAL DIMENSION OF EUROPEAN LABOUR MARKETS

Ben Roberts

Emeritus Professor of Industrial Relations,
University of London

SINCE THE CONSERVATIVES took Britain into the European Community in 1973, the Social Action Programme has been an issue of contention. At first it was simply opposition to proposed directives, such as the Fifth, that went much further than British employers were prepared to accept. In the period immediately after Britain joined, a Labour Government was in power which, whilst not prepared to take Britain out of the Community, shared the opinion of the TUC that little that was good was likely to come from the Community and not much was to be gained from actively supporting the Commission's objectives. Since the Thatcher Government has been in power this situation has radically changed. Today all parties are now in favour of Community membership, but the enthusiasm shown for the Social Action Programme by the TUC since its recent conversion is not shared by the Government.

As we have seen from the earlier papers, the issues are fundamental. The Social Action Programme promoted by the European Commission raises questions that are of major significance in relation to the objectives, structure and processes of the legislative, administrative, judicial and consultative organs of the Community, and the obligations and rights of the sovereign member-states which have created the Community by the Treaty of Rome and its functional completion by the Single European Act (SEA).

The European Community as seen by Mrs Thatcher is primarily a customs union between sovereign states which exists to facilitate the free flow of goods, services, capital and labour within and between member-states, as a means of raising levels of economic efficiency, wealth and living standards of individual citizens and institutions domiciled in the member-states, which wish to retain their own differing systems of governance and economic and social institutions.

M Jacques Delors sees the Community rather differently as an instrument not merely to promote economic ends, but like Jean Monnet, a founding father of the Community, as a stepping-stone to the creation of a democratic socialist European super state that will be able to maintain the cultural identity of European civilisation against the capitalist threat of the USA and Japan and the Communist threat of the USSR.

Differences of dogma and belief

Underlying these two concepts of the Community are differences of belief in the relative economic efficiency and ethical implications of markets and individualism on the one hand and, on the other, the economic and ethical implications of centralisation, *dirigisme*, corporatism and collectivism, as means of achieving both efficiency and fairness throughout the Community.

The Commission has defended its incursion into the regulation of employment relations on the grounds that it is in the tradition of the public law of member-states to harmonise and raise standards and that this has long been accepted through such international bodies as the International Labour Organisation (ILO), and in declarations such as the European Social Charter. It is further argued that the social clauses in the Treaty of Rome, and extended in the Single European Act, are aimed at trying to overcome inequalities in economic and social development in order to avoid economic and social tensions.

These arguments carry a certain weight, but the assumption that there is a way of determining the pattern of employment relations that is best for all the member-states in the European Community where historical experience, legal principles, and custom and practice have differed considerably could be said to be dangerously arrogant and probably more likely to create tension and division than harmony and co-operation. British employers' organisations feel extremely strongly that this is the case; so too did the trade unions until they recently had a change of mind for political reasons.

The history of the efforts of the Commission to establish a programme of social action suggests that its content has been the product of intellectual dogmatism based upon certain national experiences and beliefs drawn from the 1950s and 1960s that are far from generally agreed between member-states, or what the Commission refers to as the 'social partners', the employers and unions and other actors in the social system.

The Development of the Programme of Social Action

In the first period of the Community, from 1957 to 1972, the Commission was mainly concerned with the development of the Common Agricultural Policy (CAP); there were few examples of positive action under the social clauses of the Treaty until the end of the 1960s. The end of the decade was a period of social turbulence brought about by substantial movements of population from the southern areas of France and Italy and rising immigration from Turkey, Spain and elsewhere, the frustration of growing expectations by the slowing of economic growth, rising inflation and attempts by governments to control these developments. The Commission began to feel pressures to help find solutions especially to problems of migrant labour and the restructuring of employment that was taking place.

In 1972 a conference of heads of state held in Paris issued a declaration of support for the development of a social as well as an economic Community. Freedom of trade was not an end in itself. This declaration gave the Commission and its social affairs directorate a filip. The directorate, which was largely staffed with personnel who were strongly committed to the Commission playing a major role in harmonising and improving social welfare policies, set about the task of producing a social action programme based mainly upon ideas that were associated with the parties of the centre and the left in the six members of the Community.

Programme of social action

In 1974 the Commission submitted to the Council of Ministers an extensive programme of social action. This covered:

(a) Advancing the rights of workers, through strengthening the role of the unions.[1]

---

[1] cf. the Donovan Commission in the UK: Royal Commission on Trade Unions and Employers' Associations, *Report*, Cmnd. 3623, London: HMSO, 1968.

(b) Extension of the obligations of employers in the following fields:
  - o Health and safety at work;
  - o Minimum wages;
  - o Sex discrimination;
  - o Contract hiring;
  - o Job enrichment;
  - o Employee participation;
  - o Protection of migrant labour;
  - o Employment of the disabled.

The programme also included securing the improvement of the social services so as to erase pockets of poverty; better standards of housing for the poorer sections of communities; vocational assistance for school leavers, young workers, elderly employees and women workers. Research was called for to provide data for social indicators including studies of incomes and wealth and the effects of re-distribution. It further proposed that information should be gathered that would be useful for the establishment of public health and ecological standards. This data was seen as providing an 'essential base for policy-making in the social field' and it aimed to clarify the basic political options in relation to asset formation and their possible impact on the redistribution of income and wealth.

This extensive programme of social action—and I have not given the whole of it—was submitted to the Council of Ministers in 1974, which took note of it and declared

> 'that vigorous action must be undertaken in successive stages with a view to realising the social aims of European Union, in order to attain the following broad objectives: full and better employment at Community, national and regional levels, which is an essential condition for an effective social policy; improvement of living and working conditions so as to make possible their harmonisation while improvement is being attained; increased involvement of management and labour in the economic and social decisions of the Community and of workers in the life of undertakings'.

The Council considered that the Community social policy had an individual role to play and should make an essential contribution to achieving the objects the Commission had set out, either by means of Community measures or by the definition of Community objectives for national social policies, without, however, *seeking a standard solution to all social problems or attempting to transfer to the Community level any responsibilities which are assumed more effectively at other levels.*

'A declaration of general principles'

This declaration by the Council in 1974 in response to the Commission's social action programme remains as a basic declaration of general principles. It provides an encouragement to the Commission, which continues to develop social policies that are based upon the programme that was endorsed, but tempered by the Council's response that this was no guarantee that a Directive would necessarily be approved if it went beyond what some member-states regarded as desirable. The Community's role in the field of social policy was left as a matter of political decision that would be profoundly influenced by social trends and the response to them by governments and the political pressures of the social partners in the member-states.

In the period since the Social Action programme was first formulated the Commission has only been able to persuade the Council to endorse Directives and regulations relating to:

o collective redundancies;

o employment of disabled people;

o equal pay for work of equal value;

o equal treatment in family allowances and retirement age;

o state social security schemes;

o occupational social security schemes;

o equal treatment for the self-employed;

o mutual recognition of qualifications;

o protection of workers against carcinogens, physical and chemical agents, and noise;

o acquired rights of employees affected by company mergers.

Currently the Commission has more than 80 proposals under consideration which are either in the drafting stage or it proposes sometime to put to the Economic and Social Committee, the European Parliament and the Council of Ministers.

The 1992 Social Objectives of the Commission

The Single European Act has stimulated the Commission to endeavour to achieve advances in social policy it claims are essential to ensure that workers will secure their full measure of social benefit from the achievement of the economic objectives of 1992.

European Company Statute: The directives which the Commission would like to see in place by 1992 include three which have been under consideration for more than a decade. At the top of the list is the *European Company Statute* which would give companies tax and other advantages as Community organisations. Among other things, companies would be required to adopt a European pattern of corporate organisation, including a two-tier board of direction and management, or what other form may be approved by the Council of Ministers. They would also be required to accept a form of employee participation based upon a choice between one of the following models:

(1) a supervisory board consisting of one-third shareholder nominees, one-third worker representatives, and one-third jointly chosen by the shareholders' and workers' representatives;

(2) or based upon a choice between different schemes, subject to employee consultation, that already exist in the Community, such as the German model. But no form of employee participation need be introduced if the employees of the company signify that they are not in favour of such a scheme.

Fifth Directive: This directive, the fifth to be proposed in a series of a dozen directives relating to company law, would require all public companies limited by shares or guarantee to make a choice between a minority of employee representatives elected or co-opted onto a supervisory board; or alternatively, if a unitary board of directors were chosen, one-third of the non-executive directors would have to be chosen by the employees; or alternatively, in either type of board structure, workers could be represented through a body representing employees which could have the same rights of information as non-executive directors; another alternative would be through collectively agreed systems which would allow them to participate in the election of non-executive directors. It should be emphasised that the final form of this directive might be changed again before it reaches the Council of Ministers.

Vredeling Directive: This directive covers employee rights to information and consultation in multi-national companies. It was bitterly opposed by employers when first presented by the Commission to the Council of Ministers from where it was sent back to the Commission.

A Directive on the burden of proof in *Sex Discrimination* cases. The first draft of this Directive was vetoed by the UK in 1988.

A Directive on the rights of part-time and temporary employees (at draft stage).

Health and Safety Directives: These include directives on safety and ergonomics; health and hygiene at work (at draft stage).

Directive on Parental Leave: at draft stage.

Directive on Information and Training for trade unionists relating to technical change: at draft stage.

A social dialogue has been arranged by Jacques Delors which has led to the creation of a joint steering committee involving members of the Euro-TUC and the employers' organisation UNICE which has discussed progress and possible amendments in the European Company Statute.

Responses to the Social Action Programme

Fear is strong in Britain that the Commission's Social Action Programme will lead on inexorably to a European system of corporatism managed from Brussels by a bureaucratic Commission largely insulated from member-states by the enfeeblement of the Council of Ministers brought about by the system of qualified majorities extended by the SEA; and by the divorce of the Euro-parliament from the member-states and managed by an extremely powerful Commission supported by a weak and divided Economic and Social Council.

In some member-states, however, an argument has surfaced and received a good deal of sympathy that without a strong social action programme the wealthier countries in the Community will suffer from social dumping, namely, that Greece, Spain and Portugal, and in future possibly Turkey, which have lower labour and social costs, will enjoy an advantage under the SEA. In other words, unless the comparative cost advantages of these countries are harmonised by a common level of social costs they will gain at the expense of the more industrially advanced countries. This is a classic protectionist argument and comes ill from sections of a Community which is seeking to promote internal competition, which is giving vast sums to these countries to improve their productivity, and which would undoubtedly give more if they became less competitive because they were saddled with an increased burden of social costs.

Mrs Thatcher's Initiative to Stimulate Growth

In 1986 Mrs Thatcher, with the help of the Irish and Italian Governments, sought to limit the Commission's determination to push ahead with its grandiose ambitions by persuading the Council of Ministers to adopt a resolution calling on the Community to stimulate job creation by encouraging the growth of small companies through deregulation, and by avoiding the approval of directives that would increase the burden of social costs. This initiative received unanimous support in spite of opposition from the Commission. In the event, as might have been predicted, the Commission has done little to promote it.

After the British initiative there was a fear among European socialists that a process of weakening directives might begin. This led, when the Belgians took over the presidency of the Council in 1987, to Mr Alan Hansenne, the Minister for Employment in Belgium, now recently elected Director General of the ILO, to put forward a proposal aimed at overcoming the deadlock between the British and Delors. This idea was the establishment of a plinth of social rights which would be based on existing directives and social rights already established in the member-states, thus blocking any deregulation, but leaving further developments to those agreed by the social partners.

The rights that would be protected under Belgium's proposals would include:

o the right of trade unions to organise and to bargain;

o the right of all workers to be covered by collective agreements;

o the right of workers to receive advance notice and to be consulted on technological innovations and other changes in the structure of an enterprise;

o a ban on successive contracts;

o the right of part-time workers to enjoy normal social security benefits, and

o to be covered by collective bargaining and to have a negotiated contract of employment;

o the right of every worker to receive retraining on the job;

o measures to protect health and safety in all types of employment;

o the right to levels of pay that would enable a family to maintain a decent standard of life.

The Belgian proposals were considered by the Council of Ministers in 1987 and remitted to the Val Duchess talks which had been initiated by Delors for their examination. In 1988 the Commissioner for social policy, a Spanish socialist, who is a strong supporter of the legislative approach, indicated that the Commission had received proposals from the Economic and Social Committee which he was considering; these might form the basis of a social charter that would be applicable everywhere in the Community. The charter would give all workers the right to enjoy a decent wage, to be covered by collective agreements, social security and health protection at the workplace; information, consultation and participation rights within firms at both national and international levels; require measures aimed at ensuring the unity and values of the family; the strengthening of women's equality as regards equal training and employment opportunities; definition of standards ensuring the total freedom of mobility of European citizens with special reference to migrant workers and recognition of professional qualifications and diplomas; the right to have access to professional training and necessary leave for this purpose throughout working life.

These elements of the much longer list previously published by the Commission are now to be included in the European Charter of Minimum Social Rights which was mentioned by Jacques Delors at the Trades Union Congress in September 1988 and put forward by the Commission in 1989 for adoption by the Council of Ministers in 1990.

There is also on the table a proposal from the European Parliament for a directive that would compel all companies above a certain size to draw up and publish an annual social balance sheet which would cover a similar range of issues as the earlier Belgian proposals. These would then be the subject of discussions between the workers, the unions and management. This idea is based on corporate social audits introduced in Portugal in 1977, which the Portuguese believe to have been successful.

Effects of the Social Charter

What will finally be adopted by the Council of Ministers from this array of proposals for which the Commission is fighting is unclear, but

47

if the substance of the Social Charter were to be adopted by the Community it is evident that it would, as Delors fervently desires, greatly strengthen what throughout Europe is a declining trade union movement. The effect would, in Britain, as the TUC hopes, largely nullify much of the change brought about in industrial relations by the reforms over the past decade. What is not recognised in Brussels, or indeed in France and Germany, is that unions in most continental countries are much weaker in the workplace, and are able to exercise far less pressure on management to resist change and secure inflationary wage increases, than their British counterparts. If collective bargaining were to be extended into the board room and a system of European-wide agreements were also to be imposed, which the Commission is anxious to see achieved, they would almost certainly be followed by demands for legal enforcement. This would create the type of rigidities which had much to do with the decline in productivity in the years of great trade union power before the 1980s. Such a development would be an encouragement to wage inflation, especially in Britain, where unions with their strength in the workplace and protected by Euro-Directives on workers and trade union rights, would, as in the past, be able to take two bites of the cherry. There would also be the danger that the great advances in human resource management achieved by British firms in recent years would receive a serious set-back.

Out-of-date philosophy

In my view the Commission's philosophy of legally imposing collective bargaining at the same time as insisting on legally enforceable rights of participation would have damaging consequences for industrial relations and the efficient performance of industry. Another danger is that this type of industrial relations development would almost certainly lead on, in times of economic crises, to attempts to regulate wages and salaries by policies imposed from Brussels which would be seen as essential counterparts to the European monetary system, European central bank and the standardisation of fiscal régimes advocated by M Delors as essential concomitants of the SEA.

In the eyes of the British Government, much of the programme of social action called for by the Commission is inherited from ideas that are now seriously out of date, and have lost much of their relevance. Not only Britain, but every country in Europe, has begun to move away from the domination of *dirigiste* corporatism towards predominantly market-based economic and social policies; and in the workplace from trade union class-based patterns of conflictual collectivist employment relations to human resource management based upon flexibility, individual satisfaction in a context of co-operation, and acceptance of mutual responsibilities by management and workers.

Conclusion

What will come out of this struggle over the future shape of the European Community? There is evidence from recent meetings of experts in Brussels that there is a recognition that social policies which may be in conflict with the economic objectives of the SEA are likely to encounter considerable resistance from employers in all countries in the Community. The Delors proposals will certainly be opposed by the British Government as a dangerous shift in the direction of bureaucratic socialism and damaging to the fundamental objectives of the SEA.

Two things can be said with some confidence. One is that Mrs Thatcher's intervention in the debate on the European Community's social programme has had a radical influence over the past few years and may have come just in time to prevent the Community from turning into a bureaucratic leviathan. And, second, if there is a change of government in Britain at the next election this could make a significant difference to the future role of the Community in the field of social policy.

5

BANKING AND MONETARY CONTROL AFTER 1992 – A CENTRAL BANK FOR EUROPE?

Geoffrey E. Wood

Professor of Economics,
City University Business School

WHY DO WE NEED a central bank in any economy? We do not, after all, need a 'central grocer' or a 'central car dealer'. The usual answer to the question is in two parts. Banking systems have liabilities which are much more liquid than their assets. Under some circumstances, this can threaten the existence of the whole banking system. The central bank is necessary so that in these circumstances it can supply to the banks the means to meet these short-term obligations. It acts as what is called the 'lender of last resort'. It can do that because—and this is the second part of the answer to the above question—the central bank is always and inevitably the monopoly supplier of that in which banks' short-term liabilities are denominated—it supplies the currency which acts as the medium of exchange.

Both these aspects of the answer have been challenged in the past and are being challenged again now. These challenges need to be discussed. But it is useful to accept that two-part answer for the first part of this paper. For that traditional answer lets us understand what are on the basis of the traditional view the crucial functions of a central bank, as contrasted with those that such banks acquire incidentally; and it also makes clear the confusion behind proposals for an international central bank.

An International Central Bank?

Proposals for an 'international central bank' have been fairly common in recent years.[1] A proposal for a European Central Bank (ECB) is a limited version of an international central bank proposal.

A central bank should, on the traditional arguments for its existence, be able to supply the medium of exchange in whatever quantity is necessary to prevent a collapse of the banking system. The bank must therefore either operate over an area where there is only one currency, or, if there is more than one, it must be able to supply whatever quantity is necessary of whichever is demanded. If, for example, we already had an ECB, it would have to be able to supply DM or French Francs or Italian Lira or any other currency in the system. It would have to have the power to print *any* currency within its area.

That is why proposals for an international central bank reveal a complete misunderstanding of a central bank's basic function; for the proposals never give it that power. And that is also why proposals for an ECB as a way to European monetary union are misconceived. If we do have a common currency, then (still taking as given the traditional arguments for a central bank) we shall need an ECB. *But until there is a common European Currency there is no role for an ECB.*

Establishing that point is an essential preliminary to this discussion; for it clears the way to three basic questions. What properties are desirable in a monetary system? Are these properties more likely to be delivered by competition or monopoly? Is competition possible, or is the supply of money a 'natural monopoly'? We consider these three questions, before turning to questions of structure, incentive and behaviour.

Desirable Properties of a Monetary System

The desirable properties of a monetary system are clear, albeit implicit, in the following brief outline of monetary history.

> 'Money, monetary policy, and monetary mismanagement account for a very large part of economic instability. There has never been a significant inflation, prices rising, say, 4 or 5 per cent for two or more years without a significant increase in the quantity of money, and practically all serious cyclical depressions have been due largely to monetary mismanagement.'[2]

---

[1] See, for example, Heffernan (1987).

[2] Haberler (1983). A useful survey supporting the first part of the above quotation can be found in Bernholz (1986), and of course the classic example of the second is contained in Chapter 7 of Friedman and Schwartz (1963).

The medium of exchange should, then, be sufficiently stable in its behaviour so as to cause neither inflation nor recession. The first makes the medium of exchange less useful by creating uncertainty about what it will buy;[3] and of course the second wastes output and sometimes causes great hardship. We should, therefore, be searching for a stable money. It will not be easy to find. Indeed, the record so far is of three-quarters of a century of failure. To quote Peter Bernholz:

'The present age of discretionary monetary policies, which began in 1914, has turned out to be an age of permanent inflation. Inflation rates have ranged from low and moderate to hyper inflationary, but have scarcely anywhere and mainly only during the Great Depression been absent. It is true that countries with rather independent central banks have enjoyed lower rates of inflation (Parkin and Bade, 1978), but the long-term effects in those countries still have been substantial.'[4]

Does European integration give an opportunity to create what has been missing and wanted for seventy-five years?

Impose a Common Money?

One sometimes hears claims that a common money is necessary for Europe to gain the maximum benefits from European economic integration. This may be true. But whether a substantial *increase* in these gains would come from having a common currency, as compared to a reasonably stable set of national currencies, is very doubtful. The Governor of the Bank of England (1988) has recently set out very clearly why this is so:

'Is greater exchange rate stability necessary if the benefits of the internal market are to be realised? The short answer, in my judgement, is "no". The purpose of the internal market programme is to remove barriers and distortions to trade—in order to reduce costs, to enable economies of scale to be realised, and to ensure that trade takes place at prices that reflect underlying economic realities. In some senses the exchange rate is a price like any other. It is therefore important that it is the right price—that

---

[3] Economists sometimes analyse a 'fully anticipated inflation'. This is a useful simplifying analytical device for many purposes, but it is not a common real-world phenomenon.

[4] Bernholz (1986).

exchange rates are not fundamentally misaligned, for example. And in foreign exchange as in any other market, a fixed price is not necessarily the right price: for a fixed price cannot adjust to changing circumstances. (It is, incidentally, also true that the efficient allocation of resources requires that trade should take place at uniform exchange rates between currencies— something that is not always the case at the moment in the Community with, for instance, agricultural green rates. But to explore that subject would take longer than this occasion will permit!).'[5]

Comparison with the USA is somewhat misleading in this context. The common US dollar partly evolved as a way of increasing trans-actions efficiency; but it was also, as a common currency has been at other times in the past (Burns, 1927), a symbol of political unity.

If a common currency is to be imposed, it should be a currency which is likely to be more stable than the available alternatives. That is the criterion by which proposals should be judged; for looking at additional gains from trade that such a currency would allow is to concentrate on second (at most) order matters at the expense of first order ones.

Can we, therefore, design a monetary constitution for Europe which would bring stable money? Or is there some other way of achieving this result?

When economists are discussing how an industry is to be regulated, they distinguish between regulation of structure and regulation of conduct.[6] Both methods are designed to produce efficiency of resource allocation. The former regulates the industry so as to keep it competitive; the latter form of regulation is recommended when a competitive structure is thought to be unattainable, and is designed to produce a competitive *outcome* despite absence of competitive structure. In other words, a regulated monopoly is usually regarded as something to fall back on when competition is not feasible.

If we impose a central bank and a common currency on Europe, we are creating a monopoly, one which we would hope to regulate so as to ensure that the money it produced was stable. As the quotation from Bernholz makes clear (above, p. 53), we have not done too well at designing such a regulated monopoly so far this century. It is wise, therefore, to start by asking not how the regulated monopoly should be

---

[5] A detailed discussion of some of these points can be found in Wood (1983 and 1986).

[6] See Kay and Vickers (1988).

constructed, but whether competition is feasible. Competition within the EC can in this context be between two different types of money. There can be competing national monies, each produced by a national monopolist; or there can be competing private monies. These two varieties are discussed in turn.

Competing National Monies?

The EC will be a régime free of exchange controls internally, and so far as can be seen also externally. Under these circumstances the citizens of any one country could in principle contract between each other in any currency which was not subject to exchange control. There could be nationwide 'currency substitution'—one country's citizens using another country's currency either instead of or interchangeably with their own. This phenomenon is fairly common in the Americas. Along the US/Canadian border, the two countries' dollars are accepted, and along the US/Mexican border, the US dollar is used.

This example is a useful one. The US dollar is used in Mexico in preference to the Mexican peso. And the US dollar is used alongside the Canadian dollar in Canada, but use of the Canadian dollar on the US side is possible but rare. In both countries, the more stable currency is more acceptable than the less stable.

The same could happen in Europe. Citizens would choose to transact in whichever currency was the most stable. It would be rash to argue that one would quickly be able to pay for a newspaper at a corner news-stand in London with any EC currency. But the use of more stable currencies for large transactions and for the holding of a stock of 'readily available purchasing power' could quickly become widespread.[7]

Allowing competing national monies would thus give the consumer more choice. And, very important, it could encourage quality improvement in all the monies. To understand the latter, note that a government gets revenue from money creation. It supplies pieces of paper which cost almost nothing to produce, and gets goods, services, and titles to assets in exchange. The classic analysis of this process is Martin J. Bailey's 'The Welfare Cost of Inflationary Finance' (1956). In that paper he showed how the process of issuing money and debasing the currency gives the issuing government revenue.

There have been numerous studies of the effects of thus resorting to

---

[7] Abolition of the legal tender laws would facilitate this process.

inflationary finance.[8] But there need not be inflation to give revenue. Expansion of the money supply will do it, and there are circumstances when that will not be inflationary. These are, of course, when the demand is rising in line with the supply. This can happen if the economy is growing, and it happens also if the money becomes more attractive. (Philip Cagan (1956) noted that when the ends of hyper-inflations were in sight, there was a sudden increase in the desired ratio of money to income.)

Consider the significance of this for a world of competing national monies. Any government can increase its revenue from money creation if its money becomes more attractive. Its citizens will hold more, and so will foreigners. As foreigners start to hold more of the country's money, they are in effect paying a tax to that country's government. This would be attractive both to the citizens—who could have lower taxes—and to the government, which could cut taxes, spend more, or both, and thus increase its chances of re-election.

Competing national monies could thus work just like competing goods—consumers would get choice, and producers would have an incentive to improve their product.

The only possible difficulty would be if the EC devised some scheme to prevent the revenue from the creation of the good money accruing to its issuer. Such a scheme would remove the incentive to improve product quality.

But in the absence of such a scheme, allowing competing national monies would bring great benefits in the form of currency stability.[9] Whether the process would end with one money being used throughout Europe cannot be foreseen, and is also immaterial.

Competing Private Monies?

Several scholars have argued in recent years for the 'denationalisation of money'—for allowing competing monies to be issued by private organisations. This case has been argued by Friedrich Hayek (1978), implicitly by Lawrence White (1984), by Roland Vaubel (1986), and very recently by Kevin Dowd (whose 1988 paper contains a brief and

---

[8] See Capie (1986) for a survey.

[9] The above argument has focussed for the sake of simplicity on the avoidance of inflation. There are also pressures for the avoidance of recession. People would be cautious about holding a currency which from time to time, quite unpredictably, became scarce.

clear survey of previous work).[10] White's study is a useful one to discuss in a little detail, as doing so highlights the two main difficulties with the proposal. White studied the Scottish banking system when individual banks could issue their own notes, and there was no government money. The system was stable, the money was stable, and Scotland prospered.

What are the objections? One is associated particularly with Charles Goodhart. He has argued that the system was stable (as were others with similar characteristics) because it did in fact have access to a central bank—in this case the Bank of England, via the London money market. Without that access, Goodhart argues, the system would have been prone to failure.[11]

Even if this is incorrect (as White and some others maintain), there is another problem with the system nowadays. In the episode White studied, there were in place two constraints apparently similar but on close examination quite distinct. One constrained each individual bank. The other constrained the system. Competition constrained individual banks. They were obliged to redeem their own notes—for gold or, if desired, for those of other banks. This acted as a restraint on the rapid expansion of any one bank by the simple device of printing notes. Thus banks were constrained relative to one another. And they were prevented from expanding all together by the obligation to convert into gold.

What would provide the overall constraint nowadays? Competition could, for it would prevent the collusion necessary for banks to get together and levy an 'inflation tax' for their own benefit. The difficulty of course is getting a competitive system established. Could a sufficient number of banks be created so that the industry would be competitive from the beginning? The problem is perhaps capable of being solved.

But I would argue here that competing national monies are likely to do a significantly better job than has been done by the 75 years of non-competition since 1914 (years characterised by the presence of

[10] The proposal is certainly not new. Walter Bagehot (1872) favoured it. His recommendation that the central bank should act as a lender of last resort and have the monopoly of note issue was in his eyes second best. He favoured it only because he thought his preferred solution, private competing monies, was not feasible since by the time he wrote the British banking system was habituated to the Bank of England's hegemony.

[11] Charles Goodhart, *The Origins of Central Banking*, London: London School of Economics, 1986.

exchange controls, it should be observed). Once we see how this system works out, we can consider how to go further, and whether any significant benefits are likely.[12]

What Should the Central Banks Do?

It is now useful to suppose that the EC moves to a system of competing national central banks. That gives point to the question of what these banks should do. By this is meant not what rules they should follow to deliver stable monies—that would be a long and separate paper—but what, rather, their responsibilities would be.[13]

First, granted by assumption, they will supply the medium of exchange. This will be what any individual bank's liabilities are convertible into, on demand or after some notice period, by law.

Second, they will stand ready to act as lender of last resort. This role entails acting not to preserve individual banks, but to protect the monetary system. It involves acting as follows. Suppose a bank fails, and depositors either lose their funds, or face a lengthy period of liquidation before knowing whether they have lost them or not. Depositors at other banks see this and, even though their banks are sound, hasten to withdraw their deposits simply as a precaution. As all banks hold only a fraction of their liabilities in cash, it is conceivable that the whole banking system collapses as a result of the failure of one member of it. To prevent this the central bank discounts securities (of reasonable quality) when they are offered to it by banks, and does so without limit until the panic is over. A vivid description of a central bank acting in this way is provided by Jeremiah Harman, a director of the Bank of England at the time of the panic of 1825.

'We lent it [i.e. gold] by every possible means and in modes we had never adopted before; we took in stock on security, we purchased exchequer bills, we made advances on exchequer bills, and not only discounted outright, but we made advances on the deposit of bills of exchange to an immense amount, in short, by every possible means consistent with the safety of the Bank and we were not on some occasions over nice. Seeing the dreadful

---

[12] Roland Vaubel in a series of lucid and meticulous papers has analysed the conditions under which private money is feasible, and how it is likely to perform under those conditions. His 1986 paper is a most useful survey of this work.

[13] A readable and thorough survey of procedures for delivering stable money is to be found in Poole (1988). See also Chapters 2-4 and 8-10 of Dorn and Schwartz (1987).

state in which the public were, we rendered every assistance in our power.'[14]

The problem only exists, of course, because of limited information. If people knew the state of their own bank (by hypothesis sound), they would not panic. On these grounds, Fitzgerald (1987) has argued that instead of a lender of last resort we require publication of information. There is no quarrel with that principle. Nevertheless, the risks are so great that it seems to be worth paying the price of retaining the lender-of-last-resort role—possibly redundant, and possibly, as Thomson Hankey argued in dispute with Bagehot, a temptation to slightly excessive risk-taking by banks.[15] The cost is small and the benefit possibly very large. In institutional terms, what would be required is that the central bank have a small department charged with sampling the information gathered by banks before they discounted paper. This would give the central bank information on the quality of the names on the paper. There is absolutely no need, so long as the central bank acts as a classic lender of last resort, for it to go any further and get involved in the supervision and regulation of banks.[16]

Central banks do of course generally have wider responsibilities. Nowadays they are usually charged with regulation and supervision of the banking system. The case for such regulation must rest on the inevitable existence of externalities or inappropriate incentives.[17]

In banking one can point both to externalities and inappropriate incentives. The former exist because one bank's solvency can be threatened by the failure of another (see above, pp. 58-59). And, as a bank's management can know more about the bank than its customers can, it is possible for the bank to make risky investments without paying its depositors, its source of investible funds, commensurate returns.

---

[14] Quoted in Bagehot (1873), on p. 73 of the 1978 edition.

[15] See Gilbert and Wood (1986) for this discussion.

[16] It can be argued that there is no necessity even for the central bank to check the quality of paper that commercial banks are discounting. Commercial rating agencies can and do rate companies. They depend for their living on establishing a reputation for doing a good job. There is no reason why the central bank should not rely on their judgement.

[17] See Kay and Vickers (1988), *op. cit.* But see also Stigler (1975) for a series of essays which show that, whatever the intended purpose of regulation, it generally benefits primarily the regulated.

Neither of these provides a strong case for supervision. The existence of a lender of last resort does mean that sound banks are not threatened by another's failure. But they are not threatened only so long as they take care to remain sound—by always having good quality paper available for discounting at the central bank. And further, if the central bank discounts only at a high rate, a charge is levied for the service. There may still remain a small perverse incentive, as Hankey argued. But it *is* small, and there is a danger if central banks get involved in supervision in an attempt to eliminate it. The danger which supervision brings is discussed below.

Is information asymmetry important?

What of the second argument, information asymmetry? It is not clear there has to be such an asymmetry. Any institution which takes deposits could be required to publish balance-sheet information frequently. This would no doubt be of little interest or enlightenment to small depositors. But that does not matter—for large depositors, firms and other banks, would pay attention to it. Their doing so would soon lead to high-risk banks paying high interest. Hence information disclosure eliminates the harmful effects of the asymmetry.

Arguments related to the above have recently been advanced by Goodfriend and King (1988). In a comment on them, Phillip Cagan accepted the logic, but argued that as the costs of supervision of capital adequacy and liquidity were very small, and the possible benefits in terms of banking stability very large, it was surely prudent to pay these small costs. That is an important point, but the extent of the costs of supervision should not be understated. These include not only the resources used up—these are, indeed, quite modest. The major cost lies in the possibility that supervision is taken by politicians and voters as synonymous with approval. If the institution is supervised, it may be assumed to be sound, and there may then be great pressures to prevent such an institution from failing should it become insolvent. Acceding to these pressures would create major perverse incentives.

If an institution can expect to keep the rewards of success but not pay the costs of failure, it will invest with regard only for return, and not at all for risk—witness, for example, the behaviour of the US Savings and Loan Associations.

Hence, although Phillip Cagan's point is very telling, it is not fully persuasive. The case for banking supervision in a world where technology permits the frequent disclosure of up-to-date information is much less strong than it was.[18]

International Comparisons

Before concluding it is useful to set out for the sake of comparison a recent proposal by Neils Thygessen (1988). Thygessen sought to discover what lessons for Europe could be drawn from the history and current operations of the US Federal Reserve. He proposed the establishment of a European Monetary Policy Committee, comprising some board members proposed by the Commission and the European Parliament and five voting governors from the participating central banks. This board would have several tasks. There would be 'exchange of information' and 'joint evaluation of economic and financial developments'. It would 'formulate guidelines for national monetary policies'. Further, it would manage the international reserves the governments had agreed to pool, and would take part in international discussions.

This is plainly quite different from the competitive system outlined above. Rather, indeed, it approximates to the establishment of a cartel to prevent competition. It is difficult to appraise the scheme; for we are nowhere told why collusion rather than competition will benefit the consumer. Essentially the proposal is the basis of a design for a European Central Bank without any explanation of why we need to create one.

Behind the proposal may lie the idea that it is useful for society to agree on one medium of exchange, and that government has to impose such a medium. But the second part of that belief is false. Meltzer (1987) summarises his historical discussion as follows:

'Collective choice of a medium of exchange does not require government action or law. The history of money shows that the choice of a medium of exchange within social groups often preceded the development of governments with the power to specify the means of payment used by all parties to the exchange. Then, as now, trade extends beyond the hegemony of particular governments.'[19]

---

[18] A possibly important consideration is the nature of the society. Is it one where political pressure can readily be exerted on the central bank? Or is the bank by constitution or because political power is not concentrated relatively immune from such influences?

[19] Meltzer (1987), p. 90.

In summary, then, Thygessen's proposal is for a cartel, the benefits of which over competition he does not explain. It can and should, for the benefit of every resident in the EC, be dismissed.

Summary and Conclusion

Europe's common internal market after 1992 can bring benefits to consumers. These benefits do not, however, depend on a common currency being imposed on Europe. Closer European integration does, however, give the prospect of Europeans having a more stable money than has been widely available for three-quarters of a century. This could be achieved, not by creating a new European Central Bank, but by letting existing central banks compete. They would compete to provide a stable money which was attractive to prospective users. This would be their primary duty, along with the role of lender of last resort—unlikely to be needed, but valuable to have available. Such banks could also be charged with some minimal supervision of their national banking systems; there is a case for that, but, it must be emphasised, a far from clear-cut one.

Allowing competing national monies could bring stable money to Europe. It would do so by harnessing a force which has long been recognised as important in economics, but has also long been neglected in discussions of the supply and regulation of money. This force was vividly described by Adam Smith (1776):

> 'But man has almost constant occasion for the help of his brethren, and it is in vain for him to expect it from their benevolence only. He will be more likely to prevail if he can interest their self-love in his favour, and show them that it is for their own advantage to do for him what he requires of them. It is not from the benevolence of the butcher, the brewer, or the baker, that we can expect our dinner, but from their regard to their own interest.'

Benevolence has failed to deliver stable money. 1992 gives us a chance to see if self-interest can do so. We should let it try.

REFERENCES

Bagehot, Walter (1873): *Lombard Street*, London: King & Sons.

Bailey, Martin J. (1956): 'The Welfare Cost of Inflationary Finance', *Journal of Political Economy*.

Bernholz, Peter (1986): 'The Implementation and Maintenance of a Monetary Constitution', *Cato Journal*, Autumn, pp. 477-511.

Burns, A. R. (1927): 'Money and Monetary Policy in Early Times', Reprinted by Augustus M. Kelly, 1965.

Cagan, Phillip (1956): 'The Monetary Dynamics of Hyperinflation', in Milton Friedman (ed.), *Studies in the Quantity Theory of Money*, University of Chicago Press.

Cagan, Phillip (1988): Comment on Goodfriend and King in W. S. Haraf and R. M. Kushmeider (eds.), *Restructuring Banking and Financial Services in America*, Washington DC: American Enterprise Institute.

Capie, F. H. (1986): 'Conditions in which very Rapid Inflation has Appeared', *Journal of Monetary Economics*.

Dowd, Kevin (1988): *Private Money: The Path to Monetary Stability*, Hobart Paper No. 112, London: Institute of Economic Affairs.

Dorn, James A. and Schwartz, Anna J. (1987): *The Search for Stable Money*, Chicago and London: University of Chicago Press.

Fitzgerald, D. (1987): Comment on Heffernan in Z. Res and S. Motamen (eds.), *International Debt and Central Banking in the 1980s*, London: Macmillan.

Friedman, M. and Schwartz, A. J. (1963): *A Monetary History of the United States*, Princeton: Princeton University Press for the National Bureau of Economic Research.

Gilbert, A. and Wood, G. E. (1986): 'Coping with Bank Failures', *Federal Reserve Bank of St Louis Review*, December.

Goodfriend, M. and King, R. G. (1988): 'Financial Deregulation, Monetary Policy, and Central Banking', in Haraf and Kushmeider (eds.), *op. cit.* (see above under Cagan, Phillip (1988)).

Goodhart, Charles (1986): *The Origins of Central Banking*, London: London School of Economics and Political Science.

Governor of the Bank of England (1988): 'The Development of the European Monetary System', Speech to the 1988 Forex Conference of the Forex Club, Luxembourg.

Haberler, G. (1983): 'Money, Markets, and Stability', *Cato Journal*, Spring.

Hayek, F. A. (1978): *Denationalisation of Money: The Argument Refined*, Hobart Paper No. 70, 2nd Edition, London: IEA.

Heffernan, S. (1987): 'The Costs and Benefits of International Banking', in Res and Motamen (eds.), *op. cit.* (see above under Fitzgerald, D.).

Kay, J. and Vickers, J. (1988): 'Regulatory Reform in Britain', *Economic Policy*.

Meltzer, A. (1987): 'Properties of Monetary Systems', in Res and Motamen (eds.), *op. cit.* (see above under Fitzgerald, D.).

Parkin, M. & Bade, R. (1978): *Modern Macroeconomics*, Oxford: Phillip Allen.

Poole, W. (1988): 'Monetary Policy Lessons of Recent Inflation and Disinflation', *Journal of Economic Perspectives*, Summer.

Stigler, G. J. (1975): *The Citizen and the State*, Chicago: University of Chicago Press.

Smith, A. (1776): *The Wealth of Nations*, ed. Edwin Cannan, London: Methuen, 6th edn., 1950.

Thygessen, Neils (1988): 'Decentralisation and Accountability within the Central Bank', in P. de Grauwe and Theo Peters (eds.), *The ECU and European Monetary Integration*, London: Macmillan.

Vaubel, Roland (1986): 'Competing Currencies: The Case for Free Entry', *Cato Journal*, Vol. 5, Winter, pp. 927-42.

White, Lawrence (1984): *Free Banking in Britain*, London: Cambridge University Press.

Wood, Geoffrey E. (1983): 'The European Monetary System', in R. Jenkins (ed.), *Britain and the EEC*, London: Macmillan.

Wood, Geoffrey E. (1986): 'Monetary Integration', *Journal of Monetary Economics*.

APPENDIX

The EMS to Date

There have been several attempts to set up a European monetary system. The system we now have is 10 years old this year. It was established on 13 March 1979, following planning and discussion initiated by Roy Jenkins in his 1979 Jean Monnet Lecture. There can be no doubt that part of the motive for establishing the system was political. It was seen as a way of moving towards greater European unity—doing what is, for some bizarre reason, habitually called in work in this area 'taking concrete steps'.[1]

This Appendix outlines the economic characteristics of the system.

The EMS has three aspects. These are an arrangement for pegging exchange rates, a system of credit facilities to help defend these pegged rates, and a proposed 'European Monetary Fund'.

Exchange-rate pegging

Two exchange-rate pegging arrangements were initially considered— the 'parity grid' and the 'basket'. The first ties every currency to every other currency in a system of mutually agreed (and consistent) cross rates. The second ties each currency to a 'European Currency Unit' (ECU), equal to a somehow-weighted average of all the member-countries' currencies. The system ultimately adopted was the parity grid. This choice was based on perceptions of where it would lay responsibility for responding to exchange-rate pressure. Under the parity grid system whenever one currency moved, all other exchange rates would also diverge from their agreed level, thus creating an apparent obligation for all countries to respond. Under the 'basket' system, it was possible for one currency to move relatively to the rest without creating any divergence, apart from its own, among the mutually agreed set of rates.

The parity grid system was chosen, but with features of the 'basket' added to it. The central rates of the parity grid were defined in terms of the ECU, and the ECU served as a 'divergence indicator'—a movement by a currency away from its 'central rate' measured in terms of the ECU, when it was greater than an agreed amount, created a 'presumption' that the country which issued that currency should act to correct the divergence.

---

[1] See, for example, Peter Norman's article in the *Financial Times* of 13 March 1989.

Credit facilities: three categories of loans

Turning now to the credit facilities, it is still the case that loans to enable exchange-rate intervention are made directly from one country to another. These loans are in three categories: short-term loans, repayable within forty-five days; medium-term loans, repayable within nine months; and loans repayable within five years. The reason for dividing these facilities by maturity was that different amounts were made available at each maturity: 14 billion ECUs were available in the second facility, and 11 billion ECUs under the third. The amount available under the facility was supposedly unlimited.

In addition, loans were made available at subsidised rates to certain member-countries from the European Investment Bank and certain other Community institutions. These loans were not, however, a part of the workings of the scheme, but rather an inducement to join it.

The European Monetary Fund

The European Monetary Fund (EMF) is intended to have pooled under its authority a portion of the gold and dollar reserves of member-countries. In return, members of the EMS will receive deposits in the EMF. These deposits are denominated in ECUs, to be used in settlement of intra-EEC debt.

The ECU is thus intended to develop a role identical within Europe to that of the Special Drawing Rights (SDR) for the (worldwide) members of the IMF. Pending final establishment of the EMF, reserve pooling was carried out in the form of revolving three-month 'swaps' among the separate national monetary authorities. That avoided any question of transfer of ownership of these assets in the absence of enabling national legislation.

Two points clearly emerge from that outline of the system. First, it is manifestly intended to operate as a pegged exchange-rate régime, a European version of the Bretton Woods system of the 1950s and 1960s.

Second, it lacks provision for the replacement of national currencies in private hands by the ECU or some other supranational currency unit, and thus lacks provision for the development of a 'European Money'.

After a shaky start, the system did establish a zone of exchange-rate stability, although at the cost of considerable interest-rate variability. The system functioned largely as a D-mark bloc. This became most notable after 1983, when France largely fell in with German monetary policy. As a result, realignments have become less frequent—after seven in the first four years.

Italy is now raising questions about the system. The Italian authorities are concerned that the removal of exchange controls (scheduled for June 1990) will threaten their continued membership of the system. It is against this background, and because of recognition that there is no way for the system to evolve further, that the Delors Committee was established. Under the chairmanship of Jacques Delors, it has 17 members, comprising central bank governors and 'outside experts'. The committee was set up in summer 1988, and reported in March 1989. It assumes that monetary union must follow from the 1992 programme for the removal of trade barriers.

6

THE SINGLE MARKET IN FINANCIAL SERVICES*

Evan Davis

Research Fellow,
Centre for Business Strategy,
London Business School

Introduction

ONE OF THE MOST important individual sectors to face
Commission attention in the internal market programme is the
financial services market. This is not only because it is large—6 per cent
of Community GDP—but also because it plays a substantial role in the
development of other sectors. Moreover, it is developing technically to
a point at which the barriers of international borders seem irrelevant.

This chapter, then, looks at the Commission's goals for financial
services, what the market reaction to them is, and what serious hopes
there are for change. These issues will highlight the problems and
possibilities that the UK banking sector will face in the 1990s, and the
increasing integration of the 12 European markets. First we describe
the Commission Directives on financial services, and outline the
benefits that could result from a more integrated market. Then we
analyse the arguments concerning scale economies. In the retailing of
financial services, any economies of scale appear to be outweighed by
economies from local specialisation, and in wholesale banking, most of

---

*This paper is an amended version of Evan Davis and Carol Smales, 'The Integration
of European Financial Services', in *1992, Myths and Realities*, London Business
School, 1989.

the economies that exist have already been exploited. Finally, we outline what, in reality, might eventually determine the quality and price of service consumers receive. This will not be a mass of cross-border take-overs, but the deregulation of services within some member-states. As the British banks appear in no position to be engaging in much acquisition anyway, due to their low PE ratios, to which the market evidently attaches a great deal of importance, this is a fortunate finding for the UK banks.

The financial services which we have analysed and on which we have based our conclusions are retail banking, commercial banking, house-purchase lending, credit card provision, and insurance. We have not examined securities trading, which is already more international than the other sectors. Much of what we say, however, also applies to securities, as indeed it does to many non-financial sectors.

The Commission's Proposals

There are three components to Commission plans for European financial integration:

o free flow of capital;

o free trade in financial services and financial service companies;

o standardisation of banking technology across Europe with a view to 'interoperability'.

These three are entirely distinct from each other. We could, for example, have free capital movements but laws that nevertheless bar local banks from intermediating in other states—as is the case within the United States. Conversely, of course, we could allow cross-border banking operations to develop, without allowing free capital movements.

In economic terms, it is probably the free flow of capital which is the most important measure that could be adopted in the financial area. It is not of primary concern here, however. For the banking sector, the key Community initiative is the opening up of Europe's financial service markets with the *Second Banking Directive*. This is designed to ensure that the best available operator within the Community is providing given services in any location. This means that no government regulations should obstruct the neutrality between buying financial services from a domestic bank, buying them domestically from a local branch of a foreign bank, or importing them from abroad.

Unifying the financial services market

The change which, in theory, would merge the 12 independent markets into one market is the proposal that once a financial services company has been sanctioned to operate *somewhere* in the Community, it would have the right to operate *anywhere* in the Community. This will release various markets from being of small domestic character to being large and European. Then, through various means, several effects can occur.

The *means* by which markets internationalise result either from trade across borders of services themselves—West Germans buying insurance from Britain, for example—or trade across borders of factors of production (such as staff, corporate control and management, and even technology or product design). Thus, for example, when West Germans buy insurance from a local subsidiary of a British insurance company, they do so because capital has crossed from Britain into West Germany. Or if British building societies introduced variable rate mortgages into Belgium, then a product design would have crossed the English Channel. In each case, the flow of some factor of production would affect the local market.

Potential benefits of the Commission's plan

These means of achieving internationalisation can have any of several *effects* on the shape of local services. There may be economies of scale that are presently unrealised in any individual national market. Opening up the European market will provide a much larger potential scale, and this should either allow economies of scale to become a source of competitive advantage, or at least let a more diverse range of suppliers serve each market, giving more choice to the consumer.

A similar argument can be applied to economies of scope. There may be efficiencies from serving, say, Greece and Italy as one unit that cannot be derived from serving them as two units. By letting companies operate throughout the Community as one unit, any such economies will emerge.

A third opportunity for change through internationalisation is the prospect of new entry into uncompetitive markets. If, say, West German insurance companies enjoy cartel profits, then the ability of British insurers to poach their clients will significantly undermine the West Germans' monopoly position. Regulations in certain states prohibit certain types of financial products or innovation. When entry barriers are removed, the inhibiting domestic regulations will be undermined.

Finally, if competitive forces actually succeed, different areas of comparative advantage in different countries can be exploited by internationalisation. If the British have banking 'in their blood', it may be appropriate for them to run financial service industries in other countries. They can do this in an integrated market either because their exports will take market share from foreign suppliers, or because they will be able to take over foreign companies and run them to the high standards prevalent in Britain.

Thus, if the internal market in banking is to work, it will do so through the realisation of economies of scale or scope; through a fresh impetus to competition in the most regulated and cartel-dominated sectors; and through the provision of service by the best operators in markets that are currently protected.

Progress in liberalising capital flows

The progress of Commission measures on the financial services front is not as encouraging as progress in liberalising capital flows. The *Second Banking Directive* adopts what is known as the 'passport principle', which would actually be better named the 'driving licence principle'. It demands that each state recognise any financial institution licensed in another Community country to operate locally, as long as it does so under local rules. Thus, just as France must allow an Italian driver to drive in France as long as he does so within the French speed limit, so under the Banking Directive, France must allow anyone licensed in Italy to perform any of a set of designated financial services to do so in France, albeit under French banking rules. The licence to operate will be issued by the home country, and it will be the home country authorities who are responsible for ensuring that basic operating standards are maintained. At the same time, the host country can enforce its own operating rules.

The Second Directive, initially agreed by the Council of Ministers in January 1988, is still awaiting final adoption by the European Parliament. It will be read with a *Solvency Ratio Directive* and an *Own Funds Directive*. The necessity behind these supplementary directives is that if each country is to recognise each other's driving or banking licences, then each must set a reasonable driving test, or bank licensing standard.

The effect of the regulations should be to make European financial markets substantially more contestable. Banks will no longer face the bureaucratic obstacles of obtaining licences in every country in which they wish to operate. More substantively, they will not face many of the implicitly protective regulations that have limited their incentives to enter profitable markets—regulations such as those that impose capital requirements on their individual branches, rather than on their operations as a whole.

Line between operating and licensing rules—a grey area

The grey area of the directives is the line between operating rules and licensing rules. In Belgium, variable rate house lending is prohibited. Does that preclude British building societies who operate under UK licences from lending at variable rates in Belgium? In mortgage lending, a separate directive was under consideration, which explicitly demanded that states grant 'mutual recognition of technique' to foreign operators. The others would thus, for example, have to accept the British building societies' variable rate mortgage practice. That Directive has now been superseded by the Banking one, which covers mortgage lending as one of the designated banking activities under its provisions. But mutual recognition of technique is not explicitly laid out in the Banking Directive, which merely says:

> 'If the competent authority of the host member-state ascertains that an institution having a branch or providing services in its territory is not complying with the legal provisions in force in that member-state which are justified on the grounds of the public good [. . .] that authority shall request the institution concerned to put an end to the irregular situation.'

This does not seem to limit the powers of the domestic authorities much, and can be interpreted even more weakly when combined with the provisions elsewhere in the Directive giving full responsibility to local authorities for monetary provision and liquidity regulation. The protection to companies wanting to set up overseas, therefore, appears to come from the fact that the Directive establishes their right to operate any activity given in a list of recognised banking activities, as long as they are able to do so in the home country. But this list is rather vague. It does not specify 'variable interest mortgage lending' as one activity, for example, but 'mortgage lending'. To make clear the intent of the Directive, either the powers of the host authorities must be laid out far more precisely, or the rights of companies to enter different markets must be protected by a much more detailed list of designated activities.

On insurance, the Commission received a boost from verdicts in European court trials which held that purchases of insurance were like purchases of Cassis de Dijon, as long as the purchaser was able to make an informed judgement about the financial security of the insurance provider. Otherwise, insurance was different because, unlike a bottle of cassis, it would fail to hold its value to the buyer in the event of its provider going bust. It thus upheld the right of large purchasers to import insurance, creating a freer market in commercial sales. At the same time it also upheld the right of member-states to prevent foreign trade for small customers who, it was felt, would be less well equipped to assess the financial viability of their insurer.

These findings have now been codified in the draft *Non-Life Insurance Services Directive* which was adopted in June 1988. When it takes effect in 1992, a genuine wholesale market in 'large-risk' insurance will be allowed to develop, where policyholders are companies with more than 250 employees, or with a turnover larger than 12·8 million ECUs or a balance sheet of over 6·2 million ECUs. This approach is being followed by planned action on life and car insurance—and it is the big customer who will get legal protection when taking out foreign policies. All these measures are in addition to the freedom of establishment that apparently exists at the moment for insurance companies.

Three barriers to a unified market in financial services

In both insurance and banking, there are three problems facing the Community in its hope to gain the benefits it cites as achievable from opening up Europe's financial services. The first is that, whatever the Commission's publications might say, changes will not be as great as some people hope. Differences in national markets sometimes reflect substantive differences in national preferences and circumstances that will not go away in 1992. One can imagine why Italian motor insurance costs 50 per cent more than the average in the four lowest-priced states, apart from mere barriers to new entry in that market.

Secondly, despite the intentions of the directives, there are a plethora of other ways in which government action can inhibit entry. Freedom of entry in insurance was provided for as early as 1979, yet Eagle Star still did not find it easy to break into the Greek market: although local law demanded the apparently weak requirement that a Greek actuary sign the operating application, it was a requirement that emerged as quite strong on the realisation that there were only 10 registered actuaries in the country, and they viewed the signing of these applications as a significant source of income.

The third difficulty facing the Community in making its market effective is to harmonise the standards that are required of the different types of financial intermediaries. It would, for example, be distorting to have weaker regulation governing UCITS (the European for unit trust) than, say, life insurance. Unfortunately, arriving at uniform standards across all financial sectors conflicts with the objective of designing politically acceptable regulatory compromises across all member-states. It is clear which way this conflict is likely to be resolved.

Despite the difficulties facing the Commission in its task, and the exaggerations of the potential benefits that might accrue, it does appear that the Second Directive and its insurance counterparts promise a sensible approach to integrating the European market into one unit.

Standardised bank electronic services?

The final component of the financial services programme—although one in which they have so far taken only an advisory role—is the imposition of standards in banking technology that will allow Europe-wide use of things like cards for automatic telling machines (ATMs) and electronic funds transfer at point-of-sale (EFTPOS). The Commission's concern is that citizens should be able to travel within the Community incurring lower transaction costs than at present. It thus makes perfect sense to try to standardise bank systems across the continent. There are, however, noteworthy side-effects of the standardisation process. In particular, they tilt the balance of competitive forces towards smaller banks who would otherwise have trouble competing on the extensiveness of their network. Providing ATMs in every high street is an important, but expensive, service, that demands a widespread market presence. If customers from small banks can enjoy the large banks' machines, one of the principal economies of scale that might be derived in retail banking services is removed. At the same time, standardisation can stifle innovation in the provision of electronic banking services.

From both the consumers' and the retailers' points of view, it would probably be advantageous overall to have reciprocity in the use of each bank's cards. The Commission's proposal on this subject is to leave co-ordination to the banks themselves, with a view to formalising whatever the banks agree on in a future directive. The Commission published the 'European Code of Conduct Relating to Electronic Payment' in 1987, a document of a non-binding nature that covers issues such as consumer protection as well as pan-European topics. The banks have responded to the Commission's proposals with the 'Accord for Payment Systems', published by the European Council for Payment Systems.

Economies of Scale in Financial Services

Although there are four principal effects of unifying the European financial markets, it is the prospect of economies of scale and economies of scope that often appear to absorb most of the attention of different market participants.

In all industries, companies often seem to believe that size is a prime ingredient of success. True economies of scale can be said to exist when one large operation is worth more than the sum of its component parts. In financial services, the arguments are that there are large fixed costs to running a network of branches or agents. These can be spread over a lot of customers in large operations (although we have seen how Community technological standards could wipe out this particular economy on the retail side). Another supposed economy derives from the benefits of scale in participating in capital markets. Unit transaction costs tend to be lower the larger you are. Consumer recognition is another advantage to the large company which might expect to attract customers most easily. Finally, a less publicly stated argument, but one that is probably more important than the others, is that a large diversified company can afford to cross-subsidise price wars in one sector with the profits made in another. Insofar as price wars occur spasmodically, wiping out a few companies each time they occur, and given that entry and exit cost something, large companies can ensure that they are never wiped out in any market. This may not, however, be true for small companies, which might find a market profitable on average, but simply be unable to weather the occasional storm. Even if the power to engage in price wars is never used, the mere threat it provides can deter entry and sustain profits at higher levels than otherwise.

As well as economies of scale, it is generally supposed that there are economies of scope in financial services. The bank doing business in all major European cities will find it easier to serve clients than a similar size bank that is locally concentrated. The international bank would be better placed to serve international clients, and would gain strategically valuable information about a range of markets from its dealings abroad.

European bank mergers

Stimulated by arguments of this sort, the desire to obtain market share in the anticipated deregulated European market has spawned a small flurry of merger activity. Much of this has been within individual Community countries, particularly Spain, where the 'Big Seven' has been trimmed to the 'Big Six'; and in West Germany, where regional banks have been attempting to merge in order to compete with the big national banks. There has also been, however, cross-border activity. Since hardly any of the major Community banks are eligible for take-over—as most are stated owned, mutually controlled or too large for governments to allow foreign ownership—attention has been devoted to small or medium-size banks and joint ventures. Deutsche Bank has acquired the Italian holdings of Bank of America; it has also bought the Portuguese bank, MDM. On top of these take-overs, there have been a series of share swaps involving some of the major Community banks. Generale Bank of Belgium and the Dutch Amro bank are set to place themselves as the Community's fifth largest bank by exchanging shares in one another's international operations. The Royal Bank of Scotland is following a similar course with Banco Santander of Spain. Commerzbank of West Germany has already declared its intention of swapping shares when Crédit Lyonnais of France is privatised.

In sectors other than banking, the story is not that different. In insurance, there have been a number of attempted mergers in recent years. The take-overs of Cornhill and Equity and Law showed that even quite large companies can be successfully acquired. In credit cards, the giant deal between Mastercard and Eurocard—decidedly unpopular with many senior personnel in Mastercard—is a large merger stimulated by Mastercard's feeling that it would gain substantial advantage in its lacklustre performance against Visa by merging with a large European player.

If the market has prepared itself for banking changes stemming from newly realised economies of scale, it is pertinent to ask whether this is really the channel through which Commission proposals will be felt. In truth, the answer to this is that it will not be. It will actually be through other effects: the stimulation of competition, and the convergence of regulation towards a more deregulated norm. This is clear if one considers the three skills that determine the efficiency of a financial intermediary:

o costs of administration in executing the intermediation;

o success in appropriately aligning the risks of various borrowers with the degree of risk aversion of various lenders;

o ability to market the services offered to borrowers and lenders.

Benefits of large scale and geographical specialisation compared

As we have described, large size can make a positive contribution to performance in three ways: it can lower administration costs; enhance intermediation skills through economies of scale and research; and lower costs in marketing, because consumer recognition is a by-product of size, and recognition is half the key to sales. However, set against economies of scale as a source of competitive advantage, is the benefit of geographical specialisation:

o The administrative benefits of size can be exaggerated. Transactions between a British citizen and the bank that handles his current account may be offered at lowest cost if the bank is near enough for them not to have to make international phone calls if they need to make an inquiry. And the benefits of maintaining small transactions within a local currency are substantial for both customer and bank.

o Local knowledge is a substantial benefit in appropriately aligning risks. A Danish insurer knows Denmark better than a Dutch one. He can make better estimates of local risks than anyone else. He knows the bad areas of Copenhagen, the ones where premiums have to be high. Similarly, a Greek banker might be a better judge of a Greek citizen's creditworthiness than a West German banker.

o In a world of pre-existing national markets, where names have already established themselves, the benefit of recognition through increased size may be limited. Indeed, localisation might be a marketing advantage. The Danish insurer knows what Danish customers want, and where to find them. French customers may be happier about sending a cheque to a company located in France, and with a French sounding name, than to one in Britain.

Even putting aside the advantages of geographical specialisation, the benefits of economies of scale themselves are sometimes misunderstood. Some of the scale economies that companies believe they can exploit only really apply to relative scale within a national market. Benefits of consumer recognition, for example, are not attributable to large companies, but to companies that are large among a given pool of potential customers. This advantage of scale is not advanced by expansion abroad, which expands the pool of potential customers as well as recognition.

Arguments for scale economies ambiguous

What we see, therefore, is that the scale economy arguments are far from unambiguous. The most important distinction to draw in discussing internationalisation of financial services is that between the retail and wholesale sectors. Retail services do exhibit some economies of scale, but they, more than any other sector, enjoy economies of specialisation too. For customers, it will be almost as important to have a local office as it is for them to have a local grocer. For the foreseeable future, it will probably remain important to purchase from an agent with a local name as well. When, for example, Eagle Star entered the Greek insurance market, they suffered a severe credibility problem in persuading the Greeks to believe that they could offer higher maturity rates than local companies. The service they offered appeared too good to be true to the Greeks. On the supply side, so many of the skills of effective intermediation at the retail level require a local under-standing, that it is difficult to believe there is any advantage in having bigger units of control than currently exist. Moreover, there are not many economies of scope that accrue at the retail level across national boundaries—the volume of personal sector transactions that occurs in foreign currency is small relative to the total.

Non-retail services, on the other hand, enjoy fewer economies of specialisation, but also fewer economies of scale. This is because no very wide branch network is necessary to serve corporate clients. Geography is simply less important at the corporate level. This means that these services can be exported and imported, and do not have to be provided locally. Commercial banking and commercial insurance and reinsurance are all things that can be relatively costlessly performed across borders, along with the wholesaling functions of retail banking services. It should thus turn out that retail services remain local in their delivery, and that wholesale services are international. In practice, the two sectors already exhibit these characteristics and, particularly in wholesaling, the European market is unified enough for most economies of scale to have already been taken up.

The conduct of financial services before and after 1992 is already well established in patterns exemplified by the relationship between Gouda, a Netherlands insurance company, and Endsleigh, a British insurance retailer, aiming particularly at coverage of student possessions and travel. Endsleigh sell insurance to students in Britain, but cover them with policies that are taken out in the Netherlands. There is no doubt that Gouda would face a much harder marketing task, not to mention a harder underwriting task, if they attempted to tap the British market alone from the Netherlands. Endsleigh are partly owned by Gouda, but still find it cheaper to insure with the British Friends' Provident group in the life policy market. In essence, the value which Endsleigh creates is in vouching for the quality of a Dutch company to a lot of British individuals who never have the time to find out for themselves what the non-British companies are like. Endsleigh are marketing insurance for a Dutch company in a country that would otherwise be closed to the Dutch.

Another current example of the same phenomenon is in the credit card market. Here, there are essentially two world brands—Visa and Mastercard. Each is retailed in virtually every Western country by a local bank. The bank will run credit card services in the local currency, itself monitoring the clients it attracts. The international parent companies themselves do rather little except maintain certain features of the card networks. Local banks, then, act as retailers of credit card services. In the UK, we have even seen the credit card equivalent of the own brand, with Mastercard marketed under the name Access by the banks who choose to sell it. In Britain, there has been a tendency—not exhibited in the United States—for these retailers to be tied to one brand or another, although this is a phenomenon that is breaking down. But the degree of retail intermediation can be taken further. In Ireland, Access cards are provided through the Bank of Ireland, which is a member of the Joint Credit Council, which administers the system for British banks. The bank is locally responsible for running its service, but also benefits from administrative back-up from Southend.

Advantages of specialisation

What these two examples show is how important the advantages of specialisation are compared with scale or scope in financial service retailing, and, at the pre-retail level, how the advantages of geographical specialisation are very much smaller, but so is the importance of geographical location at all. Economies of scale also evaporate once a small minimum efficient scale is reached.

The structure of the industry is thus not determined by the magnitude of economies of scale between different companies, but by the degree of intermediation that it is profitable for retailers to provide between wholesalers and customers. Consumers would find the costs of monitoring all available operators—especially if this includes a number of foreign ones—too high, so would never consider importing their foreign services even if they could be imported efficiently. The intermediation skill is therefore to provide that monitoring. Retailers can take that intermediating role, monitoring the 'best buys' at home and abroad. It is thus they who can buy services from abroad if need be. But the retailers themselves enjoy only limited economies of scale, and will not need to be international to fulfil their role in selling services to customers.

Successful operators in an integrated financial market will be those who correctly exploit the economies of scale and scope that do exist, without sacrificing the specialisation that can also be very important. It is puzzling that economies of scale are so widely touted as a source of competitive advantage when there is so little evidence of their significance. The regional banks in West Germany, for example, are attempting mergers to place themselves on the scale of the large national banks. But they already have fewer employees per dollar of deposit, and much higher profits per employee than their national counterparts. It is odd that they should want to expand into the less profitable arena. It does seem quite possible that there are economies of scale in banking, but it also seems apparent that these are fully exploited at a size well below that of the top Community banks, a size which has already been reached by the major regional West German banks.

It is even more puzzling that banks believe themselves able to exploit economies of scale by international merger. In an economy where there is overcapacity, merger can lead to an orderly rationalisation that benefits all participants (the merged bank can have one branch in every high street rather than two, say). This is to some extent what has been occurring in Spain. But in general, merging in a static or growing market fails to exploit many of the economies that might be said to exist, economies which hold within the domestic market, but not beyond it. The regional banks in West Germany will not have a much easier time attracting new customers than any other new entrant if they expand by extending into new markets where they are unknown.

Perhaps one reason that economies of scale and scope are less important than many imagine is the increasing ease with which they can be replaced by a careful selection of well-designed vertical and horizontal corporate relationships. Just as Endsleigh are too small to carry the risks they insure, they can contract with Gouda to do so, while still keeping their comparative advantage in insurance marketing. Just as the Trustee Savings Bank is too small to run an effective international credit card network, it can do so by subscribing to Visa International. If there are economies in administration, the small banks should contract out some of their functions to large-scale specialised companies which can reap the economies.

Merger does represent one form of vertical or horizontal relationship that companies might want to consider. It is, however, only one of many, and it is by no means the best in all circumstances. For local services, it makes no very great difference who owns the local company. It will be manned locally, with local customers. For companies for which local service is not so important, export and import trade will be able to function effectively. All that owning a French bank does for a West German bank is to ensure a particularly stable export or import partnership. Certainly, this is a partnership that could involve synergies of the traditional kind that suggest economic agents should group into companies rather than act as individuals, but these benefits are of a smaller order of magnitude, and are very much more subtle than many suppose.

The Implications of the Commission's Proposals

Mechanisms for change

If economies of scale are not going to transform the European banking scene, is there any role for the Commission's proposals to play? If engaging in merger to create giant Eurobanks and insurance companies is not the way to prepare for 1992, then what is the best strategy for 1993?

Although the direct effects of forthcoming changes may not have much impact on financial services, there will be indirect effects operating through numerous mechanisms, which will enhance competition in several markets. These will be particularly evident in those markets where current performance is very poor. Change will result from the overthrow of regulations incompatible with open trade of the sort everyone in the Community purports to desire. Competition will also be enhanced through the greater opportunities for cartel-busting entry that are inherent in the Second Directive. A second source of change is that an improved environment for take-over may induce better management. And third, comparative advantage in provision of different products resides in different countries, encouraging suppliers with the comparative advantage to expand.

If benefits are to stem from the overthrow of regulations, European courts and Community governments will have to take a strong view of what the Second Banking Directive implies. It would be tempting to believe that if a directive were going to have any effect, it would never actually be accepted by the Council of Ministers, or at least would be ignored in subsequent behaviour by member-governments. However, this is too pessimistic an attitude. By putting more emphasis on certain banking regulations, the effect of the Directive will be to enhance the quality of policy-making in this area, as the regulations that will be challenged are those that make least sense. In France, for example, interest-bearing current accounts are illegal. If the Second Directive is enacted, either foreign banks will not have to adhere to the rule in the French market, in which case it will become untenable for the French to impose it on their own banks; or it will apply to foreign banks, in which case it will very likely be challenged in the courts, with foreign banks claiming that mutual recognition of technique is implied in the Second Banking Directive. The Commission would probably support the foreign banks in this claim. Whatever the outcome of such a court challenge, the very focus of attention on such a regulation is likely to threaten its existence.

The positive effects of removing regulations are not going to come from the stimulation of trade as much as from the fact that the most vulnerable regulations are usually nonsensical from a domestic point of view. The ironic aspect of the proposals, then, is that they will have their impact by embarrassing some member-states into adopting more deregulated approaches to their banking sectors. In financial services, '1992' has become a vacuous catch-phrase embodying a lot of meaningless rhetoric, but rhetoric that could be politically effective in carrying a lot of sensible measures through difficult domestic opposition. It would be quite wrong, therefore, to be dismissive of the measures that are being taken or critical of the Commission's approach. It is simply that the effects will not operate through the mechanisms outlined by proponents of the internal market programme.

Similar arguments apply to the markets in Europe that are not uncompetitive on account of regulation, but on account of cartels. 1992 throws a public spotlight on the relative performance of these sectors and even if new entry can be deterred, the mere upheaval involved in deterring it and defending the cartel might bring a more competitive air to various countries.

While the removal of regulation and cartels are the main change in prospect, if the take-over market is also allowed to develop freely, it will further its traditional function of providing for efficient management incentives through the threat of acquisition. This means that an outsider can come in and sweep away the bad management of an appallingly run company, and replace it with good directors. Although the effectiveness of take-over might be thwarted by national restrictions on take-over, and competition policy concerns, it should raise management standards in the medium-sized sector of the banking and insurance industries, and this should carry across to those companies which are invulnerable.

Finally, there is some chance that the good companies in one market can drive out the bad in others by taking market share in some form other than take-over. This, however, is not likely to result in changes as large as through the destruction of regulations and cartels. For example, the British insurance companies might appear to have a large comparative advantage over West German ones, and thus might be expected to take customers away from the West Germans, but in practice, almost all the comparative advantage is probably based on the more competitive structure of the British market or on tax advantages that British life companies face relative to their foreign competitors. Once these are accounted for, it is not clear that West Germans would want to invest through the British companies rather than their own.

Strategic Implications

All this discussion has strategy implications for those involved in providing financial services in Europe. Banks, insurance companies and house-purchase lenders will see opportunities in new Community markets that will be worth pursuing. It may be that they are more efficient than the local providers, or it may be that the local service is so uncompetitive that profitable new entry can occur. Either way, two outcomes are possible. Either entry does occur, and the local market improves as a result; or the local suppliers improve performance enough to keep potential entrants away. The amount by which a local bank has to improve its performance to avoid foreign incursion is to the point at which the advantages of its local presence just outweigh its inefficiency. There are banks in some sectors that should be engaging in improvement to that point now.

If a bank or insurance company in one market does see opportunities in another, it has three methods at its disposal to make a market presence in the new location. The first is to open up new branches. The second is to export to the market, perhaps at a low price to generate sales. The third is to buy an existing branch network through merger or take-over.

Strategies for retail banking

In retail banking, opening new branches does not seem an attractive option. In virtually all the member-states, there is perceived to be some degree of over-capacity. It is, therefore, probably cheaper to buy a bank that has already sunk the set-up costs of its branches than to buy the branches. There are plenty of branches and plenty of staff in most of the Community states. The feeling is that Spain, which has one branch for every 1,250 citizens, is particularly over-extended. In West Germany, the figure is similar, while in France and Britain it is more like 4,500.

In retail insurance, set-up costs are not nearly as large. The network effect is not with branches, but with a sales team. Most countries are dominated by sales through tied agents. Only the UK, Ireland and The Netherlands understand the concept of 'independent brokers', and even in Britain, the burden of regulation is making tied agency the only sustainable channel of sales. This gives some advantage to incumbents, although by no means an insurmountable one. Its more important impact is to make entry impossible other than on a large scale. It creates an economy of scale within the local market with the effect that it is not worth entering without a serious commitment to obtaining a substantial market share. The successful entrants into Britain have provided tied agency networks, and have gained such a share. They may not have been able to enter at all without making such dramatic inroads into the market.

Exporting appears unattractive to market participants in any retail service. It involves entering unfamiliar territory with an unfamiliar (and probably foreign-sounding) name. As we have seen, for both the customer and the supplier, the local connection is important. While services are increasingly being provided around plastic cards, and while these leave plenty of room for exports without much local presence, it will still be necessary to have a limited branch network, if only as a sign of commitment to the local market.

In retailing, therefore, this leaves small-scale acquisition as the most promising mode of entry. This provides flexibility about the size of presence to be developed, and does not entail the addition of new capacity in markets already overbuilt. It is not primarily to gain economies of scale, therefore; it is a cheap way to gather local intelligence. An example of an acquisition of the type that might become common when licensing rules are relaxed is that of Abbey National's new Spanish subsidiary, Abbeycor Nacional Hipotecario. This was a joint venture between a Spanish money-broking business and a Swiss insurance company which already had a substantial branch and agency network. This is an authentic foreign operation, lending to Spanish residents for domestic purchases. Unlike the Abbey National Gibraltar office, it is not designed to finance the Costa del Sol homes of British citizens. Although Abbeycor is not offering the full range of services available to British borrowers, it is on the innovative end of the Spanish scale. It has the potential to grow into a major force in Spain, particularly if it starts to retail savings services as well as lending ones. It is likely that Abbey National have done well not to create the trauma of a major bank take-over—something that they were in no position to pursue anyway, and would clearly never have been able to start from scratch in setting up new business.

Strategy in the wholesale market

This pattern of seedcorn take-over need not become a norm in wholesale services. As location is not the determining factor in choice of bank or insurer, there is plenty of room for exports. West German companies wanting to benefit from the much lower English premiums have found no difficulty in taking out insurance in England, albeit through West German brokers. With claims as large as those made by moderate-sized corporations, the disadvantage of having to deal with a company abroad pales into insignificance. In wholesale services, therefore, any exploitation of comparative advantage can be pursued from the security of a domestic base, possibly with a small local office.

Implications for the UK Financial Services Sector

These arguments contain good and bad news for financial institutions in the UK who have to watch their own backyard as well as ponder the merits of expanding into the rest of the EEC. While the Commission's own figures indicate that British fortunes would be at best mixed—in insurance, the UK is held to be very strong and in consumer credit very weak—and the low PE ratios prevalent in UK banking stocks foretell a period of the British providing dinner for hungry Europeans, our conclusions are that the important effects in European financial services will not be in the UK. The British already have an open and relatively deregulated financial environment. This goes a long way in removing any strong grounds for believing that strong new entry here can occur.

As for entry abroad, the low PE ratios do preclude the British from major take-over abroad, but as we do not believe major take-over abroad is likely to be a means to anything except inflexible and clumsy collaboration between units that would better collaborate flexibly, this does not seem much of a handicap. Small-scale take-over is possible, especially in the form of a joint venture, and that is likely to be the means of spreading British innovation and managing skill to the rest of Europe.

As for British consumers, it is difficult to see them losing, whatever the fate of the UK clearing banks and building societies. If foreign banks buy up the British, the best thing they could probably do with them is to leave them alone, and thus service would probably not change that much. The slightly increased prospects for new entry into the UK market that are provided under the Second Directive will certainly not increase UK margins and prices, and the prospects of banking standards being brought into line might provide a significant quality improvement for customers.

Conclusion

This discussion implies that financial services will remain local at the retail level, and be heavily export/import led at the pre-retail level. The Gouda and credit card examples are not something that will suddenly happen in 1992. They have already emerged in a market that is already fairly well integrated. What 1992 will bring is the prospect of more of the same.

The programme will have no immediate effect on the structure of retailing and wholesaling. If the Second Banking Directive is accepted in the spirit in which it has been written, it will have some effect on the efficiency with which the current structure operates. What is ironic is that this effect will not so much be from internationalisation *per se*, but from deregulation—hastened by the fact that nonsensical rules in certain member-states primarily designed to protect local markets in some form or other will be challenged. The burden of proof turns away from such regulations, and they will require far more justification in order to be sustainable.

This is an area where the Commission has not attempted an 'arithmetic average' type solution to harmonising standards. Instead, their proposals appear to leave a large role to the functioning of market forces. It is our belief that these forces will generally operate for the public good. This is not the approach that has been taken in other areas—notably fiscal reform—where more directed harmonisation has been advocated. It would be wrong to believe that market forces always deliver improvements in regulatory environments, but it happens to be the case that in financial services this will be so.

The banks who must make the forces work, however, will take time to sort out what the sources of competitive advantage are. These will not include size, and 1992 will not auger the era of four Eurobanks with branches stretching from Athens to Dublin. The parties who are most threatened by any forthcoming changes are not small banks, but those in the retail sector whose inefficiency exceeds their advantage from local positioning. The quicker they face new competitive challenges, the quicker they will adopt new operating practices to maintain market share prior to new entry. These developments will benefit the European consumer.

7

BRITISH AND EUROPEAN COMPANY LAW

L. S. Sealy

Lecturer in Law,
University of Cambridge

Introduction

WHEN THE UNITED KINGDOM joined the European Community on 1 January 1973, there was only one operative company law directive, and the scale of its impact on our domestic company law could be measured by the fact that only a single section of the European Communities Act 1972 was needed for its implementation. In those not-so-far-off days, we company lawyers talked naturally enough of 'the Companies Act' (the relatively slim 1948 version, of beloved memory): its principles regarded as reasonably well settled and tolerably comprehensible—sufficiently so, that the average small-town lawyer or bank manager could be relied on to find his way about in it, and our students could be expected to write an examination on the basis of memory—admittedly, in some cases, a rather modest memory—without any need to have access to the text.

Today, 'the companies legislation' is contained in a monster volume of 1,350 pages, which the Bill currently before Parliament will soon swell to 1,600 or more, a corpus of law so complex and intricate that not even a top-ranking practitioner or a university professor would claim that he fully understood it; and if such a person were to be asked why this should be so, it is almost certain that he would put the blame first and foremost on the Common Market and the mandarins of Brussels.

Although it may not be entirely fair to single out the Brussels bureaucrats or, for that matter, the European politicians as the primary culprits (as I shall seek to show in a moment), it is undoubtedly true that these people have played a major part in this regulatory exercise. It is also true that there are very many more proposals and draft measures at various stages of progress in the EC company law harmonisation programme, the great majority of which will undoubtedly find their way in due course into our domestic companies legislation and add even more rules to the undigested mass that we have already accumulated. In the decade from 1979 to 1989, the volume I have referred to has grown from 450 to 1,350 pages. There appears to be nothing to stop it from trebling again in the next decade—unless it is a groundswell of resistance from business itself. Of this, I think that it is just now becoming possible to detect the first faint stirrings. The question then is, if it is not already too late: What can we do about the problem, and how best to set about it?

I propose to examine a number of topics in sequence:

o the EC company law harmonisation programme: what it aims to achieve, what it has so far done, and what it has yet in store;

o the way in which EC directives have so far been implemented by domestic legislation in this country;

o the extent to which the EC programme, and recent UK companies legislation as a whole, has been regulatory (as distinct from enabling) in its thrust and nature;

o by way of comparison, a brief look at the development of company legislation in other jurisdictions, notably those of the United States, where a history of competing régimes has led to increased simplicity, flexibility and (the evidence would appear to show) efficiency;

o in what ways the EC might, even at this fairly late stage, change the direction and emphasis of its company law policy away from standardisation and towards something more on the American lines, and how we in the UK might give a lead;

o whether, in our own domestic sphere, we are thinking sufficiently along the right lines ourselves.

The EC Company Law Harmonisation Programme

The basis for the harmonisation of companies legislation is to be found in Articles 2, 3(c), 3(h), 52, 54, 58 and 220 of the Treaty of Rome. In sum, these measures provide for 'approximating' the economic policies of member-states and promoting a harmonious development of their economic activities; the abolition of obstacles to the free movement of persons, services and capital; the approximation of laws of member-states to facilitate the proper functioning of the common market; the abolition of restrictions on the freedom of establishment, including the freedom to establish and manage companies, firms and similar undertakings; the co-ordination of safeguards throughout the Community; the mutual recognition of companies or firms; the retention of legal personality in the event of the transfer of a company's base from one country to another; and the facilitation of transnational mergers.

Under the broad head of 'co-ordination of safeguards', we have seen a number of directives promulgated under Article 54(3)(g). Those which have so far been adopted, and are applicable to companies generally, include:

First Directive (68/151): Parties contracting with a company are protected against defects in a company's incorporation, limitations on its capacity, internal restrictions on its directors' authority, etc; so that people are free to deal with companies without inquiry.

There is no doubt that the removal of these hindrances to ordinary commercial dealings (in those jurisdictions where they had survived) was a beneficial reform.

Second Directive (1977/91): Companies in each member-state were classified into *public companies* and *private companies*, or their equivalent, and requirements as to minimum capital, maintenance of subscribed capital, etc., imposed, most stringently upon public companies. This is conceived of as a measure for the protection of creditors and appears to have strong support among European legislators, even though experience in other jurisdictions has shown that such protection is largely illusory, and certainly insufficient to justify the elaborate and expensive procedures that the directive prescribes.

Third and Sixth Directives (78/855, 82/891): These directives impose a uniform procedure and safeguards for the merger and demerger of public companies within the same member-state. Their object is to ensure that minority shareholders and other vulnerable groups are adequately protected. The drafting is careful and well-meant, but the whole exercise is rather pointless since in many jurisdictions alternative procedures exist which are unregulated and cheaper and simpler to adopt—for example, in the UK, take-overs and hive-downs.

Fourth and Seventh Directives (78/660 and 83/349): These directives set standardised formats for the accounts of all companies, public and private, and for the accounts of group companies. In so far as they ensure that accounts are prepared to the highest professional accountancy standards, they are not open to criticism. But they do in my view go into far too much prescriptive detail—entirely contrary to the whole idea and purpose of a harmonisation directive, which is meant to specify broad *objectives* only, leaving it to each domestic jurisdiction to achieve those ends by its own concepts and legislative machinery. As it is, approximation has been replaced by standardisation, at considerable expense to European commerce in compliance costs.

Eighth Directive (84/253): The qualification of company auditors. This directive should in due course ensure not only that company accounts are independently audited to professional standards, but that duly qualified auditors enjoy recognition throughout the Community.

Other directives, already operative, are concerned with companies whose securities are officially listed for trading on the share market. These include the directives on the admission of securities to listing (79/279), the contents of prospectuses of listed companies (80/390), and the continuing disclosure requirements for listed companies (82/121).

All of the directives described above were adopted some time ago, and most have already been implemented by member-states (some with more alacrity than others!) or are in the process of being implemented.

Directives not yet operative

On the horizon, we now have a number of relative newcomers—some already adopted, others at the draft stage or still only proposals.

A directive (87/345) was adopted in June 1987 on the mutual recognition of listing particulars, which will not only allow an EC company to seek stock exchange listing in more than one member-state without separate approvals, but also authorise the Community to enter into reciprocal agreements with non-EC countries for the mutual recognition of such particulars.

A directive (85/611) on UCITS (undertakings for collective investment in transferable securities)—better known to us as 'unit trusts' or 'mutual funds'—was adopted as long ago as 1985, but is not required to be implemented until later this year. A UCITS scheme which meets minimum requirements for recognition in one member-state (risk spreading, separation of trustees and managers, permissible investments) may be freely marketed throughout the Community.

On 12 December 1988, EC finance ministers adopted an 'anti-raider' directive, which will require a shareholder who has built up a significant percentage holding of shares in a publicly quoted company to disclose his interest (at thresholds of 10 per cent, 20 per cent, 33⅓ per cent, 50 per cent and 66⅔ per cent), and also to disclose the fact that he has at any time changed his position above or below one of these levels. This is intended to prevent secret share build-ups. A few member-states already have similar legislation, which in some cases (e.g. the UK) sets more demanding standards. The new rules will complement the existing regulations which require listed companies themselves to disclose information about substantial shareholdings.

The Council also reached a common position in December on a directive relating to prospectuses which accompany 'first issues' of company securities, aimed primarily at 'second-tier' companies—that is, those of small or medium size which have no full stock exchange listing but wish to have a measure of public equity participation.

A directive on take-over bids has been proposed by the Commission, designed to establish a framework and set of harmonised rules to regulate take-overs. Among the objects of the legislation will be: the disclosure of adequate information to shareholders, including a statement by the bidder as to his intentions for the future of the company; a ban on partial bids; a mandatory obligation to make an offer to buy the remaining shares imposed on anyone who acquires a 33⅓ per cent holding; and restrictions on the defences open to the boards of directors of offeree companies. Again, the UK has already, in the City Code, rules which go rather further than the EC proposals: the main debate, so far as the UK is concerned, is whether the Code should be allowed to continue outside a formal statutory framework.

Two further proposed directives would (i) introduce a Community-wide framework for regulating the investment service business, extending to brokers, market-makers, investment managers and other intermediaries; and (ii) co-ordinate and provide for the mutual recognition by member-states of the supervisory rules governing dealings in securities.

These new measures, when implemented, should open up the opportunities for the free movement of capital and the carrying on of investment business throughout the investment markets of the whole Community, and, by extension, also allow foreign traders and companies access to these markets on a basis of reciprocity. We certainly will not have a single market until all the proposed machinery is in place.

Supranational forms of corporation

Mention should also be made of proposals for two supranational forms of corporate organisation, the European Economic Interest Grouping (EEIG) and the European company.

The EEIG was established by a Community regulation (2137/85) in 1985, and will require to be supplemented by national law before it comes into effect on 1 July 1989. The EEIG is a new form of undertaking designed to encourage co-operation between businesses across national frontiers in the Community. The role of an EEIG is to provide common, non-profit-making support activities such as data processing, training, research, etc., and it will function with unlimited liability. All profits (and losses) will be channelled to the participant members, whose liability so far as the EEIG is concerned will be unlimited. It is proposed that an EEIG will be 'transparent' for tax purposes.

The draft regulation for a European Company Statute (ECS) would provide a supranational form of incorporation, subject to Community law. Membership is to be restricted to other limited companies, of which at least two must be subject to different national laws: in effect, the scheme provides for a form of trans-national merger. Many of the features of the new corporate form appear to have been settled—for instance, it will be subject to minimum capital requirements, be required to have a two-tier board, and provide for compulsory worker participation. Also, controversially, there is proposed a tax concession which would allow losses in one member-state to be written off against profits in another.

Some dispensations are being planned for small and medium-sized enterprises (SMEs). In company law, the most concrete proposals take the form of relaxations in the *Fourth Directive* (accounts), which for the first time recognise a separate category of owner-managed companies for EC purposes.

The greatest controversy continues to surround the draft *Fifth Directive* on the structure and management of public companies. The directive would provide for the mandatory use of either a two-tier management structure or of a one-tier board with differentiation between executive and non-executive directors; and also for employee participation in management following one of a number of prescribed forms. It would also deal with the duties and liabilities of directors and the rights of shareholders and minorities. Linked with the Fifth Directive is the 'Vredeling' Directive on procedures for informing and consulting employees. This introduction of a 'social dimension' into company law has both its passionate adherents and its implacable opponents, but pressure for the adoption of both measures is mounting as 1992 approaches.

Other proposed directives include:

o 9th directive on the conduct of groups (including the loss of limited liability in some circumstances);

o 10th directive on cross-border mergers;

o 11th directive on disclosure requirements for branch offices;

o 12th directive on single-member companies;

o 13th directive on take-over bids;

o a directive on insider trading.

Beyond general company law, there are many other proposals in the pipe-line, dealing with 'special companies'—banking and insurance companies, and so on—which are outside the scope of this paper.

UK Implementation

The UK Government has, on the whole, been assiduous in carrying out its obligation to embody the company law directives in its domestic legislation. Our record on deadlines has not been perfect, but it has been well above average. Unfortunately, most of the directives have for understandable reasons been based upon a civil-law model—in many cases that of the German code—and so it is we, as a common-law jurisdiction, who have had to make the most substantial adjustments to accommodate the new EC rules within our existing institutional and conceptual framework. It has to be said that we have not done this well. The invariable routine has been to superimpose a fairly literal translation of the provisions of the directive, as a new layer of regulation, on top of the common-law and statutory rules that we already have. This has led to adverse comment, even from such unlikely sources as France: Professor André Tunc has expressed astonishment that we in the UK now have *five* distinct layers of rules governing contracts made by a director with his company. But company advisers continue submissively to work their way through the five check-lists week in, week out, without apparently questioning whether someone should not be making it his business to rationalise and synthesise the law.

Another point that can fairly be made is that our domestic lawmakers have at times used the implementation of an EC rule as an occasion to extend a prescriptive rule more widely than the directive has required. For instance, much of the second directive applies only to public companies, but in the UK Companies Act 1981 such matters as mandatory pre-emption rights, shareholder authorisation for allotments, etc., were made applicable to private companies as well.

The Directives: Regulatory or Enabling?

Most of the thrust of the directives adopted so far has been regulatory. However, it can be argued in relation to some, if not most, that they have derivative consequences which *are* enabling. Thus, for example, the mandatory accounting formats imposed by the fourth directive oblige *companies* to follow a strictly-defined layout for their balance sheet and accounts; but this, it can be argued, enables a *third party* dealing with a company (and especially someone from another jurisdiction) to follow the accounts with ease because accounts of the companies in his home state take the same form. In the same way, the reciprocal recognition of professional qualifications, listing requirements, measures for the maintenance of market integrity, and so on, *enable* people and companies here in the UK to deploy their skills and have access to markets and opportunities throughout the Community, but only at some cost in unifying the standards that must be observed.

It thus comes naturally enough to us in England to regard the UCITS directive as 'enabling' because it will open up the whole of Europe to our established (and traditionally over-regulated) unit trust industry, and at the same time to consider the fourth directive on accounting formats pointlessly prescriptive because we have primarily relied on the extra-legal 'true and fair view'. The real question that we should be asking is not whether a measure is regulatory or enabling, but whether it is more regulatory than necessary. And if we are to see the issue in a world perspective, rather than as one bounded by the borders of the Community itself, we should be judging what is 'necessary' by world standards, too; and this surely means that we must not pursue an idealistic goal which leaves European business un-competitive by those world standards. The size of a book is a pretty crude yardstick, I know, but it is at least symbolic: I believe that if big business in North America can be run on the basis of an Act of fewer than a hundred pages, and small business in South Africa can flourish with only thirty-five, we in Europe ought to be going back to the drawing-board and asking ourselves whether, with our 1,350-page monster, we may not have got our priorities wrong.

The USA and Other Jurisdictions

It has never been assumed in the USA that there is any need to take positive steps to harmonise the company laws of the different states. The laws there allow a corporation chartered in any state to operate in every other state, and it is accepted that the law of the state of incorporation should govern all the internal regulation of the company—even if its activities are located elsewhere. A corporation validly formed under the law of any one state is recognised as a legal entity throughout the other states. There is no federal incorporation law (though there is, as we know, federal regulation of the issue and sale of securities). This situation has led to a competition between states to attract incorporations, with Delaware scoring as the outright winner in the race.

The most successful states have proved to be those with permissive, rather than restrictive, codes—a phenomenon which was originally condemned by commentators (purely on the basis of intuition) as a 'race to the bottom', for it was thought that laxity in the legislation would lead to the personal enrichment and aggrandisement of directors at the expense of investors and those dealing with companies, but which more recent empirical research has shown to have the opposite effect: investors put their money where directors can use it most efficiently, and this they can do where the law imposes the least restraint on their freedom to act. The competitive process is seen as leading to a more efficient set of corporation laws, which is driven by market forces to offer shareholders the best protection against exploitation and managerial incompetence, and thus maximise the value of their investment.

This experience strongly suggests that it is we in the EC who may have got things wrong. Here, it appears to have been assumed right from the outset that there never could be a true European common market without centrally directed measures for the co-ordination and integration of the domestic codes of company law, and the super-imposition of facilities for the creation of Euro-companies. In the United States, by contrast, 50 separate jurisdictions have throughout modern history pursued a common economic objective, whilst allowing each member-state to devise independently its own legislation for the formation and regulation of corporations and their commercial activities; and such inter-state harmonisation as there has been has been driven by market forces, not by centralist theorising, as one state has vied with another to persuade capitalists and investors alike that it is offering the legal environment best calculated to encourage enterprise to flourish. We in Europe, who have accepted a persistent augmentation and standardisation of regulation in the name of 'company law harmonisation', are in serious danger of rendering our continent internationally uncompetitive, as the relatively unimpeded corporations of Delaware and similar jurisdictions get on with their merchandising, undistracted by the array of procedural 'safeguards' and bureaucratic formalities which we Europeans accept so un-questioningly as an inevitable concomitant of incorporation.

Earlier, I mentioned South Africa in the context of small companies. The Close Corporations Act introduced there only three or four years ago is a model code of commendable clarity and brevity which any government which was seriously interested in offering deregulation to its small businesses could study with great profit. It is already being copied in Australia. The radical nature of the new South African close corporations régime can be seen by listing the features which we take for granted that have either been abolished (shares, capital, directors, annual returns, registration of charges, filing of accounts) or made optional (meetings, majority voting, audit). Membership is restricted to a maximum of 10 natural persons. Limited liability and corporate personality are accorded in return for little more than an annual certificate that the company has a professional 'accounting officer' who confirms that it has kept accounts to acceptable business standards.

Over 60 per cent of small businesses are now incorporated under this new legislation, and another 30,000 are joining in every year. I wonder how many of the self-styled 'deregulators' among our government spokesmen have read or even heard of this imaginative—and successful—innovation?

A Change of Direction in the Community?

The adoption of the Single European Act and the impending arrival of 1 January 1993 has now focussed minds upon the urgent need for action to make a single market a reality, and the call on all sides is for 'deregulation'; but this is seen far more as a matter of the dismantling of frontier controls, etc., than the liberalising of company laws. The best sign to date has been the proposal to relax the accounting requirements for small and medium-sized enterprises, which even goes so far as to suggest that it should be made *mandatory* in all states not to require small companies to submit to a professional audit.

But elsewhere, the negotiators seem locked in the customary battles, taking their familiar stances on the time-honoured issues. Worker participation is stalling progress on the Fifth and Tenth Directives and the European Company Statute, with the UK cast in the main obstructionist role; Germany will not allow the EEIG corporate personality because of the tax and other implications of its own domestic laws; there is pressure from some states and resistance from others in regard to the removal of limited liability when a group company becomes insolvent; the UK wants to keep the take-over panel a self-regulatory body when other states contemplate no half-way house between no regulation at all and a full statutory régime; and so on.

A Change of Heart by the Legislators in the UK?

It would be easier for the UK negotiators to argue for their EC counterparts to join them in taking a radically different approach if there were some signs that in the reform of our domestic company law we were doing the same. But here, all the Government talk of deregulation has not been matched by action. It is the same Government avowedly dedicated to the promotion of enterprise that has been responsible for the whole of the massive growth in companies legislation that we have seen this decade. The Companies Bill currently before Parliament is almost entirely regulatory, like its predecessors— with more rules, more licensing, wider investigatory powers, more

99

enforcement agencies, new and increased penalties. The abolition of the *ultra vires* doctrine recommended by Dr Prentice becomes a 'refinement' of considerable intricacy, extending over many pages; reform of the law on the registration of charges may save the cost of 30 civil servants, but will create untold bother in the registered office of every company in the land, for a parallel but wholly inconsequential registration régime must now be set up there; the promised 'elective régime' for small businesses adds up to five minor concessions. And now that the EC is urging the abolition of the mandatory professional audit for the small companies, it is the UK, contrary to the wishes of its own accountancy profession, which is sticking out against change. There is no real sign that the call for deregulation in company law has begun to be taken seriously in this country.

This is a matter for regret, for here in the UK, behind and beyond the stepped-up regulation which we have seen in the 1980s, is a company-law tradition of tolerance, flexibility and self-regulation— much of it sharing the same common-law roots as the US régimes— from which the EC member-states as a whole could learn some most valuable lessons. If we are to match our rivals in the trading world in competitiveness, I am convinced that more has to be left to the business judgement of directors, the professionalism of company secretaries, advisers and auditors, the remedial powers of equity and the common law and the creativity of the judges, and the discipline and competition of the market; far less to the prescription of the legislators. However, we have a long way to go, both at home and in the wider context of the Community. It would be the greatest shame of all if we were to end up taking lessons in deregulation from our European partners.

The best way forward, I believe, apart from putting our own house in order, is to press for businesses in the Community to have the widest range of options. For this reason, there is nothing about the European Company Statute that anyone needs to fear, for it has already been agreed that its use shall be optional: if a British firm does not like the notions of a two-tier board, etc., that are to be enshrined in its provisions, there are plenty of other ways by which a cross-border merger can be effected, independently of Community law: Shell and Unilever demonstrated this long ago. We are not far short of the position where a company incorporated in any EC jurisdiction will be free, as in the USA, to base its operations anywhere that it chooses. I believe that it would be worth our while to make considerable concessions in order to achieve the adoption of this one single rule—even if it meant accepting the Fifth Directive (which, as regards worker participation, has now reached a much watered-down form). That could be the beginning of a competitive process between one EC state and another by means of which, with enough imagination and sense of purpose, the UK could truly become the Delaware of Europe. We already offer shelf companies on competitive terms to businessmen in half of the Community: let us build on that.

THE AUTHORS

Victoria Curzon Price is British and the daughter of a diplomat. She went to school in the UK but travelled widely as a child and feels at home in many countries. She studied at Geneva University and the Graduate Institute of International Studies in Geneva, where she obtained her academic degrees. There she also settled down, married, and had three children, kept sheep, dogs and horses and a kitchen garden—and embarked on an academic career.

Her thesis, entitled *The Essentials of Economic Integration* (Macmillan, 1972), was about the European Free Trade Association (EFTA). Here she claimed that freeing trade was 'the essential' element in trying to create an integrated economic space and that harmonisation (then being pursued with enthusiasm by the European Economic Community) was not necessary. Strangely enough, this theme is once more to the fore, this time as official European Community policy. Her 1988 Wincott Memorial Lecture, *1992: Europe's Last Chance? From Common Market to Single Market* (published by the IEA as Occasional Paper 81) charts some of the implications of this 'new approach' to economic integration.

Her other published works cover international trade and commercial policy, European industrial policy, employment issues and the renewal of the European economy.

Victoria Curzon Price is Professor of Economics at the Institut Universitaire d'Études Européennes (University of Geneva) and Visiting Faculty Member at the International Management Institute, Geneva.

Sir Ralf Dahrendorf, Hon. KBE, FBA, has been Warden of St Antony's College, Oxford, since 1987, and was previously Director of the London School of Economics and Political Science, 1974-84, and a Governor since 1986. He was born in Hamburg in 1929 and educated at the University of Hamburg, 1947-52 (Dr Phil 1952), and the LSE, 1952-54 (PhD 1956). He has taught at various universities, including Saarbrücken, 1957; Palo Alto, 1957-58; Professor of Sociology at

Hamburg, 1958-60, Tübingen, 1960-64, and Konstanz, 1966-69. He was Parliamentary Secretary of State, Foreign Office, W. Germany, 1969-70; Member, EEC, Brussels, 1970-74; Professor of Social Science, Konstanz University, 1984-87. Visiting Professor at several European and North American Universities. Reith Lecturer, 1974. Member of Royal Commission on Legal Services, 1976-79, and Member of Committee to Review the Functioning of Financial Institutions (Wilson Committee), 1977-80. He has been awarded honorary degrees by numerous universities.

Sir Ralf's many publications include: *Marx in Perspective* (1953); *Klassen und Klassenkonflikt* (1957, English trans. *Class and Class Conflict*, 1959); *Essays in the Theory of Society* (1968); *Plädoyer für die Europäische Union* (1973); *The New Liberty* (1975); *Life Chances* (1979); *On Britain* (1982); *Law and Order* (1985).

Evan Davis is currently a Research Fellow at the Centre for Business Strategy (CBS), London Business School. He was previously at the Institute for Fiscal Studies (IFS) and has engaged in consulting for clients in Britain and the United States. He is joint author of *The Penguin Dictionary of Economics* and has published papers for the World Bank, as well as writing reports on professional services, exchange controls and VAT for the IFS and CBS. He has degrees from the Universities of Oxford and Harvard.

Sir John Hoskyns has just (July 1989) retired from the position of Director-General of the Institute of Directors, to which he was appointed in July 1984. Born in 1927 and educated at Winchester College, he served in The Rifle Brigade, 1945-57 (Captain). IBM United Kingdom, 1957-64; founded John Hoskyns & Co. Ltd., later part of Hoskyns Group Ltd. (Chairman and Managing Director), 1964-75. Head of Prime Minister's Policy Unit, 1979-82; special adviser to the Secretary of State for Transport, 1982. Knighted 1982. Director of companies, including ICL, 1982-84; AGB Research, 1983-89; Clerical Medical and General Life Assurance Society, 1983-; McKechnie, 1983-; Ferranti International Signal. Hon. DSc Salford University, 1985.

B. C. (Ben) Roberts was born in Leeds in 1917. After working in a variety of occupations he obtained a trade union scholarship to the London School of Economics. From there he won a scholarship to New College, Oxford. After graduating in PPE he was awarded a research scholarship at Nuffield College and a part-time lectureship at Ruskin College, Oxford. From 1949 he has worked at the London School of Economics as Lecturer, Reader and from 1962 to 1984 Professor of Industrial Relations. He is now Emeritus Professor.

He has been Editor of the *British Journal of Industrial Relations*, which he founded, since 1963.

He has been sometime visiting Professor at universities in America, Europe and Commonwealth countries, and consultant to the International Labour Organisation, OECD, and the EEC amongst other bodies.

Professor Roberts's many publications include: *Trade Union Government and Administration in Britain* (1956); *The Trades Union Congress, 1868-1921* (1958); *Workers' Participation in Management* (1972); *Reluctant Militants* (1972); and *Industrial Relations in Europe: The Imperatives of Change* (1985). The IEA published his *Trade Unions in a Free Society* (1959, second edn. 1962), and his Wincott Memorial Lecture, *Mr Hammond's Cherry Tree: The Morphology of Union Survival* (Occasional Paper 76, 1987).

Dr L. S. Sealy was born in New Zealand, studying and practising law there for some years before going to Cambridge for post-graduate study (1952-58; PhD 1958). He returned to Cambridge in 1959 and has taught law there for the past 30 years. He is a Fellow of Gonville and Caius College, and a University Lecturer in Law. He has specialised in company law and commercial law, and is the author of several textbooks, including: *Guide to the Insolvency Legislation* (1986); *Company Law* (for students, 4th edn., 1989); (joint ed.), *Benjamin's Sale of Goods* (3rd edn., 1984). Dr Sealy has also advised in the drafting of companies legislation for Malawi and other developing countries.

Geoffrey E. Wood is Professor of Economics at the City University Business School. He has taught at Warwick University and been on the research staff of both the Bank of England and the Federal Reserve Bank of St Louis. He is co-author of *Financing Procedures in British Foreign Trade*, and co-editor of, among others, *Monetary Targets, Financial Crisis and World Banking System* and *Macro-Economic Policy and Economic Interdependence*. He is Economic Adviser to Union Discount Company of London.

Professor Wood has been a member of the IEA's Advisory Council since 1987. He was co-author (with Gordon T. Pepper) of *Too Much*

Money . . . *?* (Hobart Paper 68, 1976), and has contributed to other IEA Papers, including a Commentary in *The State of Taxation* (IEA Readings 16, 1977), *Could Do Better* (Occasional Paper 62, 1982), and *Agenda for Social Democracy* (Hobart Paperback 15, 1983).

The State of the Economy

The State of the Economy

An assessment of Britain's economy
by leading economists
at the start of the 1990s

Tim Congdon
Walter Eltis
Jonathan Haskel
John Kay
Giles Keating
David Lomax
Bill Martin
Patrick Minford
Gordon Pepper
Bill Robinson
Introduced by Graham Mather

At the start of the 1990s, the British economy has reached a paradoxical juncture. The 1980s saw the 'supply side' dramatically improved with the performance of former nationalised industries transformed, industrial relations recast and share ownership widened. Tax rate reductions and privatisation policies became a model for economies throughout the OECD.

Today these achievements are overshadowed by the re-emergence of some traditional British economic problems, many rooted in the question of 'sound money'. It is disturbingly clear that economists and policy makers have *still* to achieve an effective system of monetary measurement and management, capable of functioning in deregulated financial markets without exchange control.

The fundamental importance of a stable monetary framework must head Britain's economic agenda in the 1990s. The distinguished contributors to the IEA's book, *The State of the Economy*, focus sharply on elements of Britain's performance, measured by international trade and productivity, as well as on the labour market and the performance of the education and training systems.

The State of the Economy is based on papers delivered at a recent major conference held by the IEA and is recommended reading for all concerned with Britain's economic prospects in the 1990s.

THE LEADING UK ECONOMISTS CONTRIBUTING INCLUDE:

TIM CONGDON	● **European Monetary Integration in the 1990s**
WALTER ELTIS	● **British Industrial Policy for the 1990s**
JONATHAN HASKEL AND JOHN KAY	● **Productivity in British Industry under Mrs Thatcher**
GILES KEATING	● **What Went Wrong with UK Demand and Trade Performance? How to Put it Right?**
DAVID LOMAX	● **The British Economy and Current Weaknesses**
BILL MARTIN	● **The Current Account Constraint**
PATRICK MINFORD	● **The Labour Market: False Start, Strong Follow-Through and Now for the Finish**
GORDON PEPPER	● **What Went Wrong? How to Put It Right? Monetary Control, Past, Present and Future**
BILL ROBINSON	● **The Keys to Success: Consuming Less and Producing More**

INTRODUCED BY GRAHAM MATHER

IEA Readings 31 ● xii + 140 pages ● 22 tables ● 40 charts ● Paperback £8.95 ● Cased £14.95

THE INSTITUTE OF ECONOMIC AFFAIRS
2 LORD NORTH STREET,
WESTMINSTER, LONDON SW1P 3LB
TELEPHONE 071-799 3745